52 Ways to Help Homeless People

52 Ways to Help Homeless People

GRAY TEMPLE, JR.

OLIVER
NELSON

A Division of Thomas Nelson Publishers
Nashville

Published in Nashville, Tennessee, by Oliver-Nelson Books, a division of Thomas Nelson, Inc., Publishers, and distributed in Canada by Lawson Falle, Ltd., Cambridge, Ontario.

Printed in the United States of America.

Library of Congress Cataloging-in-Publication Data

Temple, Gray, 1941–
    52 ways to help homeless people / Gray Temple, Jr.
        p.   cm.
    1. Homeless persons—Services for—United States.   2. Voluntarism-
-United States.   3. Social service—United States—Citizen
participation.   I. Title.   II. Title: Fifty-two ways to help
homeless people.
HV4505.T46   1991
362.5'574'0973—dc20   91-2236
                                                             CIP
ISBN 0-8407-9594-7

            1 2 3 4 5 6 — 96 95 94 93 92 91

Contents

Acknowledgments

I would like to thank Anita Beaty of the Atlanta Task Force for the Homeless for reading the manuscript and for offering helpful suggestions, criticisms, statistics, and encouragements. Inasmuch as our two outlooks differ to some extent, however, responsibility for the finished product is mine alone. I also am grateful to Victor Oliver, my publisher, for his help throughout the project.

Introduction

The following suggestions will help you make a measurable difference in the lives of people who don't have homes. They are practical—even the ones that may strike you as playful.

Not all of these suggestions are easy. Some of these are time-consuming. Others require enlisting the efforts of other people who may or may not pay attention on the first pass. Many of them will result in emotional upheaval, mostly yours. Nevertheless, they are within your grasp. People like you have done every one of them. You don't need special skills to do any of them. You don't have to be smart, rich, religious, expert, or especially brave. Yet, they will matter to people.

The fifty-two suggestions fall in a deliberate sequence. They begin by getting you acquainted with some homeless people before any efforts at helpfulness begin. Once you know some real people, the suggestions lead you through personal experiences in the field and some research projects. Though nobody is out of the shelters so far, you will already have enriched some lives. Equally important, you will have increased your eventual effectiveness as someone who knows what the situation is, what will help, and what won't.

The concluding suggestions require the cooperation of other people.

Though it is assumed that you will pursue these more or less in order and on your own, a group of friends can use these suggestions in a collaborative effort, dividing up the research projects, for example. A club might use them as an annual project.

Four outcomes will result from your working with some of these suggestions. First, you will accumulate a lot of information you didn't previously possess. Second, that in turn will affect your thinking about the problems of people without homes. Third, your compassion will deepen. Fourth, you will slide off the spectators' bench and step into the action.

Before you get started, though, some preliminary considerations will enrich your experience and enhance your effectiveness. Let's limit them to four.

First, keep a private journal of your impressions as you get involved with homeless people. Record what you are learning, the new questions occurring to you, growing hunches, and your feelings about everything. Above all, record *stories*. Stories are the real life of the countless numbers and tables and statistics you will encounter from time to time. Stories are the life of the people this whole thing is about.

If you possibly can, keep the journal strictly private. It's for you alone, not for posterity. If you make the rule that no eye but yours will ever see a word of it, the journal will serve you better. In the event you want to share a portion of it with another person for any reason, embrace the discipline of copying out the applicable section.

Second, right up front you will be instructed to get to know some real flesh-and-blood homeless people. You may feel tempted to do some study before getting close to the folks. That is a *great* mistake. Your study and research aren't going to be reliable—not even safe—unless you can reflect on what you're reading or hearing through the lens of actual relationships. Those relationships will help you detect nonsense, a certain amount of which is floating around the issues of homelessness.

It's also easy later on when you get involved in some of the systemic aspects of the crisis of homeless people to drop your dealings with the actual people. That is another *great* mistake. Those friendships keep you honest and ensure that your efforts are meaningful.

If the pursuit of any of these suggestions pulls you away from an actual meeting with a street person, delay following the suggestion and make the meeting.

Third, resolve right now to delay being helpful until later in the process. Thinking of yourself as being there to help is a way of anesthetizing yourself against the experience. Just be there. They don't need permission to be downtown; neither do you. You require no excuse to get to know these people. And if you can be with them with no immediate outcome in view, you will quickly come to enjoy and love them.

Fourth, you cannot expect street people to change in response to knowing you (although some of them will) if you are not changing in response to knowing them. Your personal growth in this project is not a self-indulgence. Don't let anybody tell you it is. It is the necessary qualification for being with the folks on the streets.

Each of those four considerations is difficult in its own way. But if you will abide by them, your life will be enriched and so, eventually, will be the lives of persons you befriend.

Where did all these homeless people come from? Aren't they with us suddenly? What accounts for their appearing in such numbers?

In the course of this project you will answer those questions for yourself. But just to get you started, here are some generalizations.

Several populations are sharing the streets, the shelters, and the soup lines.

Deinstitutionalized mental patients are out there in great numbers. In 1980 there were five hundred thousand public mental health beds in the United States. Today there are fewer than one hundred thousand. In recent years civil law has brought patients' rights to the point that it is difficult to keep someone hospitalized against her will. Idealism suggested local communities could accommodate mental patients better than state hospitals had been doing since new psychotropic medicines can make them more docile than previously. (So far, few have made the trial.) Short-term political practicalities directed more public funds to other projects and less to mental hospitals. The result? Many former mental patients occupy the jails. The streets are filled with disoriented people with nowhere to go and no one to make them take their psychotropic medicines. A new cottage industry (rather literally), the personal care home has developed to take in some of these people—the ones, that is, who have some checks (Social Security, disability, veterans' benefits) coming in monthly.

Some persons use the streets and shelters to get their bearings while they case a new town for work—rather like American students in Europe use youth hostels. Many will get off the streets as soon as they pick a direction. A minority are traditional hoboes. Most of these individuals (primarily males) want to get inside as quickly as they can.

The population of addicts represents another group. If they are forty years old or older, their drug is probably alcohol. If they are younger than forty, it's usually crack cocaine. A high proportion of these men are combat veterans. Many have wives, families, and children in other cities with whom they cannot live.

Women who have children and who have been divorced, have fled abusive spouses, or otherwise have fallen below the economic line so that they are unable to pay for a dwelling make up the fastest growing element of the street population. This group will suffer the worst consequences because the streets ruin children's chances at a productive life.

Seeing whole families—complete with father/husband—on the streets is no longer unusual. If a dual-income couple loses one income, the whole family may lose a home.

Some common elements recur in these otherwise different populations.

Many already have jobs. They just don't make enough to afford housing at today's costs. Many experts believe that the homeless problem is primarily a housing shortage. The Department of Housing and Urban Development (HUD) says that a household should pay no more than 30 percent of its monthly income for housing. HUD's estimate for "fair market rate" on a single-room apartment in urban areas ranges from $450 to $600. It follows that more and more working people cannot afford the going rent rates for very long before an illness, accident, or delayed paycheck gets them evicted. It may be more complicated than that, but it's certainly no less complicated than that. More low-cost housing would largely clear the streets.

The longer people are on the street, the more discouragements they face, and the more likely they are to get caught in the crack economy. Crack cocaine is a special retreat for these people. It's hard not to want to step into it from the street. It does not turn people loose easily. It follows that the sooner we can help people back into houses and into productive, safe work, the sooner their children can get into safe day-care programs, and the less time crack has to grab them.

All of them are on the street because something about the existing human community did not bear up under their weight. That should concern us all. If it can't carry their weight, can it carry ours? We should seriously consider the answer to that question. We all have a stake in repairing the tears in our social fabric. Remember these words of the poet John Donne: "Never send to know for whom the bell tolls; it tolls for thee."

1. Get to know some homeless people

Background

Getting to know some homeless people is the hardest step of all.

What makes it difficult is the fear homeless people stir up in us. Most of us aren't scared of personal harm from these folks; it's a more subtle fear.

- We're embarrassed around them.
- We have a lot of questions, but we think we may hurt their feelings if we ask them.
- We don't want to raise false expectations, appearing like Lady Bountiful or Daddy Warbucks.
- We're shy with new people in general.
- These people seem at home in a setting that is foreign to us (streets and alleys).
- Suppose that person were *me* or someone I love?

As odd as it sounds, those fears make it important for us to get to know some homeless people before trying to do anything helpful.

All kinds of projects for their relief will occur to you within minutes of getting into conversation with them. But you must realize that these initial ideas may be suitable later. Right now, at the beginning, they are self-protective ways of justifying your presence there. They seem to give you something to do (like boiling water when a baby is unexpectedly on the way in your very living room).

If you can screw up your courage, decide to be bumptious, and sit down next to a homeless person with no set agenda other than getting to know each other, you're well on your way to becoming part of the solution.

Homelessness is a symptom of the breakdown of human community. Sitting down to enjoy another person's company is the very foundation of community. Help comes later. Relationship comes first.

How to Do It

Go where homeless people can be found. Suggested places include

- shelters
- soup kitchens
- public health clinics
- park benches
- libraries
- bus stations

You may prefer to volunteer at a facility if you need an excuse to be there to get talk started. But consider trying it without an excuse.

Don't mind getting stared at. Homeless people have time on their hands and nothing much to lose. Staring at you breaks the monotony.

Be frank about your reason for being there. You've heard there are a lot of people without homes in your locality and want to get to know some of them. Ask if it would be all right to talk together awhile.

Don't apologize for your life-style, clothing, auto, or the like. Your proper entitlement to them constitutes a hope that homeless people can share for themselves.

A one-shot visit is okay; it's better than no visit. Don't promise to return unless you actually plan to. Consider the benefit of a longer-term acquaintance with the people you select to talk to.

Remember that if these first relationships are to bear fruit, you should not present yourself as a resource to be exploited. One experienced poverty worker remarked, "There can be no authentic talk with people when there's a checkbook between you."

2. Learn to enjoy some homeless people as persons

Background

Human beings were designed to live in community. The most nourishing basis for community is love. Homelessness is a result of the breakdown of community. So love is a missing ingredient.

So far so good. But what kind of love are we talking about? The word *love* is overused and misused, often applied to situations and relationships you wouldn't want to be involved with.

Try this disarmingly simple definition of love: *Love is the experience of pleasure in a relationship.* If you enjoy being with somebody, chances are that you love the person. If you don't enjoy being with somebody, try using some word other than *love* to describe your actual relationship.

Back to homeless people. The trick is to *enjoy* your new friends. That's love. It restores human community. For now, let other people see to their sheltering, clothing, feeding, and health, as inadequate as those services must seem. (You'll be helping out later.) Your task right now is not to incur their gratitude. It's to get to like some of them.

This point about enjoyment is much more important than it seems. Homeless people are accustomed to having people like you stare through them, avoid catching their eyes, and walk on past. They come to know that they are invisible to most of us. If you enjoy the company of homeless persons, you give them the gift of knowing that somebody realizes they exist. That's at least as significant as food and shelter.

How to Do It

Liking other persons and having them like you involves

- shared enjoyments
- conversational relaxation

To share enjoyments, explore some of the recreational activities that most vicinities offer at no charge, such as public concerts, amateur sports events, public art displays, public drama displays, and park openings. Pick something so that your friend does not have to be your guest. If your friend can suggest an activity, he or she will have that much more mutuality (read, dignity) invested in the relationship.

To relax in conversation, claim freedom early on in your talks to joke, to ask questions, to say no. (There is nothing for either of you to lose. It's a heady freedom, isn't it?) Make it clear that your first couple of noes are not signals that the relationship is over. You are creating space for real relationship and promising the restoration of the community that human beings cannot live without.

3. Stop saying "victim"

Background

This suggestion is tricky. A common way to avoid a social problem is to blame the victim, to think that the individual had it coming, so as not to feel personal responsibility. And homeless people are often victims of forces they do not control, such as

- the cost of housing versus take-home pay
- an estranged husband who will not pay child support
- a new freeway that levels the only low-cost housing near job sites
- a factory closing

The problem is that seeing people as victims can dehumanize them and make them seem too different from yourself. This kind of perception subtly stimulates the breakdown of human community because for all of its intended sympathy, it still divides humanity into classes of "them" versus "us."

The real currency of wealth as opposed to poverty is not so much money as it is *options*. Rich people (us) have lots of options. Poor people have fewer options. As long as you know you have some options, you are not yet destitute. Thinking of homeless people as victims blinds us—and them—to the options they retain.

Accepting the idea that homeless people retain some options (even if you haven't spotted many yet) keeps them in the fold of "people like us." As a result, our conversations with them are immediately more dignifying and eventually more helpful.

How to Do It

For the next few days, listen for people's options in all your conversations. (Caution: I said "listen," not "explain to them." If you fall into the explanation trap, you'll wind up being "it" in endless games of "Why don't you?/yes, but. . . .") Learn to be aware of people's strengths rather than their weaknesses, their gifts rather than their defects.

Sure, it sounds Pollyannaish. But that habit characterizes people who are most effective in their dealings with homeless people, so do it anyway. You're just relating to them the way you'd relate to other friends.

After you become good at the habit of listening for people's choices, options, strengths, and resources, listen to your new friends that way. Show your pleasure each time you hear your friends acknowledge personal options.

For example, the person might say, "I could check the paper for regular construction jobs and quit going back to that labor pool." "Umhmmm," you respond. Just that. No need to be patronizing by adding, "That's a *great* idea!" Your simple acknowledgment of the choice builds community.

Later we'll discuss some conversational strategies to help your friend make accurate decisions. Those strategies depend on this habit. Stop seeing your friend as a victim. Recognize that your friend is empowered with options.

4. Break the guilt habit

Background

You may be tempted to avoid poor people because you feel guilty around them. After all, you're doing well enough to be able to shop in places where this book is found. Look around that store next time you visit it. How many homeless people do you see?

The economic jury is still out, debating whether or not your being well-off amounts to stealing from poor people. Ultraliberals say yes; ultraconservatives say no way. But if you interpret that uncertainty as personal guilt, you'll simply avoid homeless people. That avoidance deepens the rift in the human community that homelessness symptomizes.

In fact, studies show that very few Americans of any economic class seriously resent the existence of the classes above us. Few of us would want everything evened out. Though our sense of fairness insists that the beginning line of the race be even (democracy), few of us expect the finish to be even (egalitarianism). The actual existence of wealth for many people constitutes hope. To many individuals, friendship with wealthy people feels like prestige.

So don't let embarrassment about being better off keep you from befriending some homeless people.

How to Do It

The principle here is the same one your wealthier friends employ when they invite you to their resort cottages or take you out on their boats. Got it?

Except for an experiment we'll describe later, don't dress down or hide the fact that you're well-off. View your material goods as means of friendly generosity. Your nice car is transportation when your friend needs it. Your telephone is a great resource for your friend because few phone lines are available for people who don't rent them.

Not only are these gestures of real service to homeless friends, but they dignify them in at least two ways. In their own street society, their prestige is sometimes enhanced by knowing you. More important, the reality of your friendship is a tissue binding the human community together.

5. Stop seeing these people as a problem to be solved

Background

The lack of affordable housing for poor people is a problem that we can solve. But homeless people are people, not problems.

This one is all background; there's not much involved practically in getting it done. You just have to change your thinking. That's not hard if you're pursuing some of the other practical suggestions.

Stop seeing homeless people as a problem to be solved? This suggestion can confuse you if the whole object is to help. Paradoxically, you are most helpful when you quit focusing on being helpful.

Well, what do you focus on if it's not being helpful? You focus on mutual enjoyment and friendship. For a long time in your dealings with street people, that's all you'd better attempt.

The reasons for that are threefold. First, if you're there only to help, you are a resource to exploit rather than a potential friend. Be sure not to confuse the two. You'd better believe that street people who survive know that distinction quite well.

Second, helpfulness is patronizing. It diminishes the humanity of the one you're trying to help. If homelessness is a symptom of the breakdown of human community, helpfulness perpetuates that breakdown.

Third, helpfulness signals your own fear. How many doctors, counselors, or ministers do you know whose nonprofessional relationships are few and catastrophic? Lots of them don't know how to manage a socially horizontal relationship, insisting that their relationships stay vertical—that is, they remain safely "on top" as helpers. Those folks may have to do that, but you don't.

If homeless people aren't a problem or a separate race, what are they? They are people. They are opportunities for friendship and new experiences. Some of them can make it back into stable life-styles; others either cannot or will not. If they are perceived as problems, we will be selective in our responses to them, trying to figure out who can make it and who cannot. This is the social equivalent of emergency room triage.

6. Start greeting homeless people in public

Background

When economically privileged people dress down, empty their wallets, and spend time on the street as "poor" people, that experience is called a *plunge*. When suburban people on a plunge experimentally dress as street people, loneliness is the pain they most often report. "Nobody *looks* at you," they tell us.

This writer once spent a week on the streets of his own city living among homeless men. During that week, he was passed (or served food!) by eleven friends who failed to recognize him.

To be sure, that's the way we live normally with everybody. We're accustomed to looking past grocery clerks, parking lot attendants, traffic cops, receptionists, and so on. Maybe it wouldn't hurt to start looking some of them in the eye as well, just as practice for the hard stuff.

In one of his many novels John D. MacDonald had his character Travis McGee notice that a sullen teenager strode into a house past her mother with no more interest than a possum in a forest pays a turtle, as though they were members of different species. Again, homelessness is a symptom of that sort of decay in human community. Looking people in the eye, greeting them, and acknowledging that fellow creatures belong to the same species are beginnings toward community restoration.

How to Do It

This one is simple. Whenever you're out in public and pass a person you assume is homeless, make eye contact, smile, and say, "Hello" or whatever casual greeting characterizes your region. (That your greeting need not set you up for a hit will be discussed in the next section. Most homeless people are no more panhandlers than you are.)

7. Ask panhandlers for handouts

Background

I think they call this chutzpah in some circles. It's important to be able to do. Asking panhandlers for handouts is not the same as taking coins out of a blind man's cup. Rather, it is insisting that community is a two-way street. There can be no real human community in which some always give and others always take. That notion dehumanizes everybody.

Well-off people (us) who are going to spend time with homeless people need this sort of skill. Remember how significant we said it was earlier to be able to say no and not have that end a relationship with a street person? Asking for a favor from a street person is part of the same principle.

The more you dwell on eventually trying this out, the more you will feel a sense of playfulness welling up inside you. All real community needs this playfulness if it is to be based on real love. As you recall, real love is not very different from enjoying another person. Playfulness, enjoyment, love, community—these all fit together. The people who work best with poor people have this quality. Burned-out poverty workers have lost it; they are too serious to get anything done that you'd want to be the recipient of.

How to Do It

Go downtown and walk around someplace where street people hang out. Catch people's eyes, and greet them. You won't have to wait long before someone walks over to you with a hand outstretched.

Now, ask him to give you a cigarette. No joke. Request a cigarette. It doesn't matter if you're not a smoker; there is no way he is going to part with a cigarette for you. (In the un- likely event he gives you one, take it, pocket it, and explain that you're going to save it for later. He has no right to insist that you smoke it his way, right then, because it's a *gift*.)

A variant maneuver is to ask for bus fare. If you get it (you won't most of the time), pocket it gratefully, explaining that you'll use it later.

If following this suggestion seems too difficult, simply ask directions of someone who seems to be a street person and let a conversation start from that point.

8. Stand in line with street people

Background

Spending a few hours in lines with street people will make you the equal of a sociologist. You will gain an appreciation for the forces and (occasional) choices that put people on the street. You will absorb their humor, their good spirits, the jauntiness they must maintain to ward off illness and human predators. You will get a sense of their real options.

As your interest in homeless people grows, you will be drawn to advocacy projects: calling the attention of other people to their plight. That is, you are going to become *political*. Don't let that word put you off. It's just the Greek word for "citizenship."

To become politically effective, you need more than statistics; you need stories. If the public safety net beneath the poorest citizens could be withdrawn by the widespread telling of a few stories of dubious accuracy (welfare queens, etc.), maybe we could get a net back in place by telling some accurate stories. But to do that, you need to have some stories. To have them, you must hear them. To hear them, you need to hang out where they can be heard—a lot.

How to Do It

First, identify some locations to visit or to be a volunteer. These would include

- soup kitchen lines
- health clinic waiting rooms
- welfare offices
- city court
- public libraries
- bus stations

This is done most simply by setting aside some time and going to one of those places, getting a soft drink to nurse, and striking up conversations. This is not hard to do. Do what you would do in starting conversation with anyone—"Where are you from . . . ?" Don't be embarrassed. The ones you are talking to are not there because they are stupid or "bad."

In one variant of this exercise it's unnecessary to dress down. Go as you are. But a useful tip in many of these exercises is not to be too jolly at first; get your mood low and sort of sullen. Believe it or not, that's how to get a conversation going with somebody who feels different from you. The normal tendency when you are with another person is to be bright and cheerful, signaling how friendly you are, how neat you'd be to talk to. People's natural reaction to this manner is to clamp shut as though you were a salesperson. But if you get your mood a little bit below theirs, they feel more comfortable about talking with you.

This strategy works with poor people, members of another race, and people of another age bracket. Go where homeless people have to be and use it to absorb stories. If you talk low-key, not all pumped up with cheer, many will converse with you at a high level of sophistication.

9. Stand in line as a street person

Background

This is a hard-core variant of the previous suggestion because people like yourself driving by are going to look at you as though you were one of "them." That's not easy the first time you try it.

The exercise gets you closer inside the story of a street person. Yet, you cannot really feel like a street person as long as you have a bed to return to tonight; thank God that you are blessed in that way. Nor can you pass for a street person very long—at least not among street people themselves. But you can go through food lines, and you can be addressed by nurses, receptionists, clerks, and bailiffs as if you were riffraff. That in itself proves instructive and will make you forever an advocate of less fortunate people.

How to Do It

Dress up to the waist in old clothes after placing them on the ground and treading on them; be especially attentive to making your white socks much less than white. Before dressing above the waist, rub unscented baby oil into your hair.

You will look as though you haven't shampooed in a couple of months.

Rub your scalp, face, neck, arms, and hands with wet coffee grounds. Let them dry, then brush off the visible grains. Now dress from the waist up. Wear no jewelry or watch. If you need glasses, get a cheap pair from a drugstore. Wear your oldest running shoes. Be sure not to use aftershave, perfume, or scented soap.

Next, go to wherever street people hang out. Talk as little as possible. Your costume makes you invisible, but your voice will betray you.

Your invisibility will serve two purposes. First, the people around you will carry on unself-consciously. Second, people like yourself will look right through you. That can be quite a jolt the first time you experience it. But as your new friends on the street will tell you, you can get used to anything.

10. Help your street friends with problem solving

Background

Though some street people in a laudable attempt to take responsibility for their lives will insist that they got where they are by their own choices, it is often more accurate to understand that they got there by *not* making choices. We all know people who got into financial trouble by "choosing" to buy a boat or a new house with an extremely high payment, to take a cruise someplace, or to vacation in an exotic location. As we listen to them describe their situations, we realize that they got stuck by not recognizing that they could afford braces for the kids or a new boat—but not both. They got into trouble by not choosing.

Often they didn't choose because they didn't know how. Choosing is a high-order mental function. In lab experiments scientists have observed that they can immobilize animals by placing them exactly in the middle of two equally attractive food sources. We should not be surprised that not all people are equally good at making choices and decisions. Nor should we be surprised that skill at decision making gets a person to the top while the lack of skill at decision making presses an individual toward the bottom.

One of the most valuable gifts you can offer your street friends is to assist them in decision making.

An important subspecialty of problem solving is conflict resolution. It is similar to the matter of helping your friends with decision making. In fact, some street people have difficulty facing conflicts. In view of the discomfort most of us feel about conflicts, that is not in itself surprising. But four additional factors make this particularly difficult for some street people.

First, they have no privacy. There is none to be had in the shelters, the soup lines, or the labor pools. People who must live in those conditions tend to close in on themselves rather than face conflict. Otherwise, where would it end?

Second, persons on the street feel little undergirding in a conflict. They are, after all, low-status people.

Third, some of the people on the street either are or have been addicted to drugs. Drug addiction suspends their emotional and social development, making it unlikely that they will respond to a conflict very imaginatively. It also reduces their tolerance for opposition, resulting in a conflict style that consists of fighting or fleeing prematurely.

Fourth, many street people come from homes where physical and sexual abuse was pronounced. That background produces adults with unclear personal boundaries. Such a child grown to adult years feels no entitlement to stick up for herself. A setting in which anger sloshes around may risk exploding long-suppressed childhood angers. Someone who was abused or violated as a child displays little skill at self-protection. The helplessness, the apparent docility, will frustrate you until you understand that condition. You'll see a lot of that on the street, not all of it limited to women.

Helping people cope with interpersonal conflict can make a difference to the quality of their lives.

How to Do It

Think of this suggestion as being similar to the old adage about giving people a fish and teaching them to fish. If people are hungry now, you give them a fish now. Teaching them to fish is a mid- to long-range goal.

Let's start short-range, with how you help your friend make a pressing decision. Unless you want your friend calling you at all hours wanting advice, be careful to avoid direct advice giving. The really elegant way of helping is called exploratory listening; you ask the right questions until the decision forms itself in the mind of your partner.

You don't ask questions off the top of your head. You already have a strategy. It's called Situation/Options/Consequences, and it goes like this:

1. Ask questions that get information from your friend about the situation he's in. Keep going until you think you understand it, usually going on a bit longer than your impatience desires.

2. Ask your friend to suggest as many options for action as he can. Encourage joking at this stage. It limbers up the right brain hemisphere.

3. Go back through the list of options—including the jokes—and ask your friend what consequences each option would probably produce.

4. Now ask your friend to choose the combination of consequences he wants, and ask him to put together a combination of options that will produce it.

5. When faced with Hobson's choice—all the choices are equally undesirable—ask your friend which outcomes he can live with the longest.

You can easily keep that strategy in your head, and it will kick out the questions you need to raise. Because your friend answers the questions, he does the work and gets the satisfaction when it pans out.

Longer-range teaching can be based on having used that strategy successfully a couple of times. "You remember when we talked about your deciding which job to take?" is a natural lead-in for a more abstract conversation about decision making as a discrete learnable skill.

An extremely helpful thing to do is to play checkers, chess, or bridge with your friend. Each of those games limbers up decision-making skills.

In helping with conflict skills, consider that we're not talking about teaching people boxing or knife fighting. We're talking about a type of decision making, of problem solving.

For many homeless people, the development of skill in addressing conflict depends on some prior developments.

First, a person needs a clear sense of personal boundaries. This idea may come as a new revelation to your friend, that such a thing is possible or permissible. But everybody has a right to feel and act self-protectively when personal space is being crowded. Discussing your own struggles with this issue can help. You probably *have* struggled with this in your life if this paragraph makes any sense to you. Just because your friend may be bellicose, don't assume that he is any good at boundary awareness. If he were better at it, he would be less combative because he wouldn't let himself get cornered so often.

Second, a person needs to think through some ways of alerting others to the effect they have on her. Often giving simple feedback to another individual will defuse tension floating in the social air. Having a repertoire of responses already thought out is beneficial. Use the Situation/Options/Consequences strategy here.

Third, people need to be good at self-mastery in conflict. For some, walking away and breathing deeply do it. For others, counting to ten achieves the same result. Whatever your friend cultivates, the object is to get out of the part of the brain involved with fighting, fleeing, feeding, and so forth and into the part of the brain that lets him play and exchange nurture. People who develop that brain skill hang into conflicts longer and more fruitfully than others.

The incidence of walking off recently acquired jobs, senseless fights, depressions, and turf battles that complicate street life can be reduced as people get better at facing conflict. Whatever help you supply will enrich their lives.

11. Discourage discouragement

Background

Discouragement is natural. Everybody feels it from time to time. But hanging on to it is bad for people in at least two ways.

First, discouragement impairs clear thinking. It's difficult to make careful decisions in the face of discouragement. As you will have noticed by now, your street friends can't afford more obstacles to clear thinking.

Second, discouragement is a health hazard. Discouraged people have lowered immunity to illness. In fact, that probably accounts for the jauntiness and swagger of some of the people you've met on the street. That manner is a survival tactic, keeping them emotionally buoyed up against flu, infections, and the like.

Your task is to discourage discouragement.

How to Do It

Don't get gushily cheerful, assuming that your attitude will cheer people up. It won't. It shuts people down and puts them on their guard. The best immediate response to self-pity is true pity. People wouldn't have to pity themselves if those around them would help out with it; self-pity is a signal that the human community has broken down in this immediate vicinity. Get your own mood low, close to your friend's or even below it. As noted in a previous discussion, that actually assists conversation with people who seem closed to it. Encourage the person to express what's on her heart and mind.

Be extremely clear that it is not up to you to solve the problem. If you think you have to rescue your friend personally, you'll be so anxious about how you're going to do it and how much it'll cost that you'll be no use whatever.

You may even agree with your friend to the point of suggesting that her situation is worse than she has said. People often respond to such suggestions by listing their actual resources and abilities. Nobody likes to look hopeless.

As you match your mood to hers and pace your speech to her speech, gradually begin joking. This beginning seems sardonic but will move to playful in due course. Your ultimate object is to help your friend gradually move into her capacity for playfulness. When somebody is in touch with that zone of her functioning, she is reimpowered.

12. Be frank with your friend about punctuality

Background

You will discover that you and your street friend do not share common values about time and its use. You wear a watch; you have a clock on your dashboard; you have alarm clocks at home; you punch a time clock at work either figuratively or literally. Punctuality is important for you. Not only is lateness discourteous, but it makes you miss planes and dental appointments.

Your friend, on the other hand, may seem quite casual about punctuality. If you make an appointment for a particular hour, you may be lucky to see her that very morning at any hour. That's enraging, especially when you're going to a lot of trouble to be present to your friend. Your thoughts are readily pulled toward prejudicial stereotypes.

The difference in time use is one that both of you came by honestly, though. (Your friend may previously have shared your sense of time. Even now she may have to rise at 4:30 to get to a labor pool by 5:00 A.M.) If you lived on the street, it might not take you long to get into that mind-set. On the street, time is your enemy. Time is something you have to kill. It's what keeps you from being able to eat midafternoon (unless you pocketed an extra sandwich in the soup line). It's what closes the (warm and dry) public library before the evening shelter is open. Besides, you don't have a watch anymore. Getting anywhere from somewhere else takes up a lot of it. Under those circumstances you cannot afford to stay time sensitive; you'd go crazy. Losing your temper in traffic is a luxury of the rich.

Yet if street people are going to make it back into the economy, they simply must embrace and submit to its schedules and its time values. The course of friendship is to be realistic about that.

How to Do It

There are no tricks to this one, except perhaps learning to be patiently impatient. You insist on punctuality from your friend. You remain punctual and reliable. You stress that that's the way it has to be. As in most situations, it's okay to joke about this. After all, most people know instinctively that jokes are based on serious points. It doesn't matter that your friend jokes with you about your uptight middle-class ways (in fact, it would be a good sign that you're friends). But the serious point is that employers are going to insist on punctuality. Putting somebody who lives on street time into a time-clock job has the same long-term promise as sending that person to the moon in a raincoat.

13. Work on language skills

Background

By now, you have long since noticed that most of your street friends are as bright as you are—as long as they are in an area of personal strength. They are good at surviving, they are experts at finding shortcuts, and some of them could have taught psychology to Freud and Jung. Some of them can charm you with their gifts of expression. (Your back-home friends have probably been startled by expressions that you inadvertently slip into your conversation from downtown.) It would take a lot of time and probably some professional expertise to recognize that even bright people can suffer the effects of limited language skills.

These days a preschool teacher often discovers that a child does not know the colors or the numbers. No matter how natively intelligent that child may be, that child has a handicapping condition. He or she will not be able to perceive what everybody else perceives. It's like missing a sense, like being blind or hearing impaired.

Wonderful results have been reported from adult literacy programs that involved helping people develop their abilities to make and vocally describe distinctions, such as long/short, round/square, smooth/rough, heavy/light.

The fact that your friend uses poetic phrases and idioms or knows twenty synonyms for *steal* can cover vistas of linguistic undevelopment. As language skills improve, so do thinking skills, decision-making skills, and employability.

Assisting your friend with that really helps.

How to Do It

Begin by asking if he wants help with reading. To your and his amusement, your friend may prove an expert in Proust or quote you a Shakespearean sonnet. It happens.

Experts in literacy development use drills that you can get them to teach you if your friend will receive them from you. A simple one involves opening a jumbled desk drawer and asking your friend to take out an object that's round or long or heavy.

But a simpler matter—and a less patronizing approach—is your speaking accurately. In so doing, identify the person you're imitating; it's probably a teacher or a relative. People imitate others when they want to be good at what their models are good at. So be somebody your friend can imitate.

Try to quit saying, "Know what I mean?" as an excuse for being precise. The more you practice, the better you get at this without sounding stilted.

Now start getting your friend to describe events, objects, experiences, and feelings. Press for precision. Let that be a habit; it's a habit that will serve him well in all settings.

14. Help your friend manage money

Background

Your homeless friend does not experience money the way you do. You budget it. You save it. You deposit it. You invest it. You assume it makes you safe.

Your homeless friend doesn't have enough money to budget without despair, so he likely doesn't budget at all. He doesn't have it long enough to save it. Nor does he deposit it. Scavengers hover around him when he gets paid; they know what he makes and they know his appetites, his needs, and his vulnerability. They will sell him some dope or some flesh or steal from him long before he gets close to a bank. Besides, he gets paid after the banks are closed, and he works during the hours when they are open. Money doesn't make him safe. It sets him up for temptation, exploitation, theft, and/or mugging. In that frame of reference, getting rid of it as soon as possible really does make sense.

You can be a lot of help to your friend in financial matters. His ultimate reentry into the economy depends on somebody doing this with and for him.

How to Do It

First, obtain your friend's permission to open a bank account. See that he gets the largest checkbook he can safely store at his shelter or leave with you. (You don't want him walking around the streets with it on him.)

You can serve him by depositing his money for him—at least a specified amount at each pay period. Be sure to get to him quickly when you know he's being paid. He won't have the money if you wait a couple of days.

Assist him with balancing his checkbook and teach him the habit. Help him resist the temptation to withdraw it all and mess up, or words to that effect.

Keep reminding yourself that if you lived his circumstances, you'd be as casual as he is with money. So be patient. He will be—that's for sure.

15. Find out what "welfare" really pays for

Background

There is a lot of loose talk about America's being a welfare state. Ironically, people who talk in those terms normally do not refer to farming corporations that are being paid not to plant crops, homeowners who receive tax breaks on the interest they pay, or the wealthy who benefit from loopholes that permit them to pay the least taxes. No, they assume that the government supports poor people at so lavish a level that drawing, as drawing welfare is called, actually beats working. They assume it works out so that women get paid to have illegitimate babies. This talk fuels our resentment against the poor.

Though nobody—not the recipients, the administrators, or the taxpayers—likes the present welfare system, our discussion of public policy is not improved by ignorance of its actual provisions.

How to Do It

Call your local welfare office (listed under county or municipal government) and ask for materials on what the agency pays. Also request names of additional agencies that assist the poor. Expect to find the employees pleased with your interest. Here are some questions to ask:

- What is the average length of a family's stay on Aid to Families with Dependent Children (AFDC)?
- How much does a family of three get?
- How does a person qualify for food stamps? How are they used?
- What rent assistance is available?
- What medical assistance?
- How soon after you go "off" a program like AFDC do other benefits cease?
- Who pays for child care if you want to work?
- Who tends your children while you look for work?
- What percentage of welfare recipients get into public housing?
- Why might a welfare mother be reluctant to take her family into a public housing development?

Playing around with the budget you would have to live on if your family were on AFDC is a bracing tonic for much of the public discussion of welfare.

16. Use a Bible concordance to look up references to poverty

Background

For reasons rooted in our history, religious Americans have to filter out a strange notion about poverty if they are to be true to their Jewish or Christian heritage. The strange notion is that wealth is a sign of God's favor while poverty is a sign of God's disfavor. Thus, the natural tendency to blame the victim takes on the cast of religious doctrine in the U.S.

If you believe that—even partially—your charity will be accompanied by a disgruntled and disapproving sigh. That's not very good for friendship with a homeless person or with anybody. It further corrodes the human community.

Most American religious thinking bases itself on the Hebrew and Christian Scriptures—the Bible. For people who imagine they know what the Bible says about any number of topics, actually *reading* in it normally comes as a great surprise. ("The Bible is a great book," said a professor. "It sheds so much light on the commentaries!")

How to Do It

Most modern Bibles have a small concordance section. You look up a word such as *poor, poverty, widow,* or *orphan,* and it gives you the books, chapters, and verses in which the word appears. You then turn to those sections to find the contexts.

Church, synagogue, and public libraries have larger concordances in their reference sections.

Many computers now run Bible concordance programs and will print out all references to a given topic.

Read the references all at once. (It will take a while.) What attitude do you discover? Does the Bible hold the poor to blame for their poverty? Whose responsibility are they? What are the consequences for ignoring that responsibility?

Our spiritual roots on this topic are worth reclaiming for our society to remain humane. If we publicly claim to be chosen people, some attention to the Chooser's commands may bear fruit in our national life.

17. Volunteer in a soup kitchen

Background

Soup kitchens are emergency expedients. Nobody thinks of them as the solution to anything. We would set them up automatically in a city that had been hit by an earthquake or some other natural disaster. How would we react if they were still in business five years later in such a city? That's an absurd idea. Everybody knows that soup kitchens are just for emergencies. Yet, many of our cities contain several soup kitchens that have operated for over a decade.

Local businesspeople hate them. They attract people who repel shoppers or clients. These businessfolks maintain that soup lines enable street life as an addictive life-style.

Do soup lines enable people to stay on the street? No question about it. Their patrons will often tell you as much. Crack addicts will work a couple of days in a labor pool, spend their wages on crack, then "chill out" for several days, rebuilding their strength on the nourishment from soup kitchens.

But try to imagine a modern city without them. Some people would starve or succumb to hypothermia without them. In one sense we can say that we have soup kitchens in order to be the kind of people we want to be. So learn what they feel like by volunteering to work in one.

How to Do It

Discover where soup kitchens are found in your vicinity. Any church or synagogue office can give you a list since most of them are run by religious groups. Or your town probably has a coalition for homeless people who can direct you.

Call during operating hours (early midmorning may be best), and ask how you can volunteer. You may want to go with a friend if the thought is daunting. Try to stick with it until it becomes a regular part of your life.

As you become more informed about homeless people and more involved in their issues, it's easy to lose touch with the people themselves. A regular morning at a soup kitchen keeps you grounded.

18. Volunteer in a night shelter

Background

The case to be made for and against night shelters is similar to that for soup kitchens. They are for emergencies. They are not a solution to the housing needs of the poor. They exist to keep people from dying of hypothermia. It is a national disgrace that they should be a regular feature of the urban landscape.

Like soup kitchens, they come under withering fire from merchants near their locations. They are said to attract riffraff to the neighborhood. A case could be made for that—with or without the term *riffraff*. It is less clear that they attract drifters from out of town. Many surveys reveal that the guests at night shelters are primarily local people. Again, it is said that they perpetuate a dependent life-style. Again, some of their guests will agree. One meets people—mostly males—who acknowledge living on the streets by choice.

Go to a shelter and find out about who uses it.

Shelters vary by clientele. Some are for single men. Some are basically for single men but have another section for single women. The latter manifest some interesting social dynamics for the curious student of shelter life. Some are for women, nearly always with one or more children. There's some poignancy to such shelters, especially as you play with the children, wondering what chances they have. A few shelters take in whole families. You have not ever really encountered grieved embarrassment until you have talked to an assortment of husbands in such shelters.

How to Do It

Again, most shelters are run by religious congregations or orders. Call churches and synagogues for the names and phone numbers of some shelters in your vicinity.

It's a good idea to try several different types of shelter. Obviously, you can consult your original sources for shelters of a different type. But keep your ears open at the shelter you're most familiar with. You will hear talk of others. Not all such talk will be flattering, human nature being what it is. People who think the town's problem will be solved if only women with children get shelter tend toward being unsympathetic about providing facilities to shelter the men who impregnated them.

Try to determine if the religious beliefs of the sponsoring group make a discernible difference in the services provided. Sometimes they do. How many different political/social philosophies express themselves in sheltering? That can be interesting.

Shelters tend to develop thick procedure manuals. You can't tell how much is really necessary until you've spent some time there. Also, shelters vary in their requirements. In some you simply check people in, feed them, doze lightly all night, fix coffee and breakfast, supervise cleanup, and leave. In others, you're a cop pure and simple, breaking up fights, expelling disorderly guests, calling 911 several times a night for all you're worth.

After a time, though, you will notice that the thickness of the procedure manual has an unfortunate impact on the guests. It infantilizes them to have so many rules and so much supervision. So it's worthwhile that somebody like *you* be a volunteer. After all, you're losing your fear of street people, your sense of difference from them.

You're starting to like them.

19. Visit homeless people in jail

Background

Though the law does not say so, a deeply held conviction in America is that only people with conspicuous property have civil rights—and the more property, the more rights. It is likely that you have received any number of mere warnings in circumstances where a conspicuously homeless person would have been arrested, notably pertaining to trespassing.

Trespassing, littering, and indecent exposure (i.e., relieving their bladders outdoors) are frequent grounds for arresting homeless people. Such arrests pick up frequency when your town is being scouted by some industry or the advance men for a convention. Word will "come down" that the homeless population should not be in evidence downtown during a given week. And you won't see them in public that week. They are in jail. Those who don't get jailed pick up on the message quickly and lay low.

How to Do It

Shelter operators and soup line operators can furnish you with lists of names of people who have been arrested at any given time and the location of the jail itself in many cases. You call the jail and ask when you may visit a certain prisoner. Don't expect to have to be too pushy. Your speech will identify you as someone who knows she or he has rights. You will be given a time.

At the beginning of your visit, find out how much time you have; your friend will know. Ask for his story, how he got arrested, how he is being treated, and so forth. Don't assume that you know in advance how the prisoner feels about his experience; don't lead the conversation emotionally. You are there to learn, not cheerlead or mourn.

What's practical about visiting homeless people in jail? Consider two effects. First, the city fathers (or mothers, as the case may be) will benefit from hearing that people like you are starting to show up at jails asking about homeless detainees. After all, they think they are serving people like you, and until you start evincing interest in these people, they pretty much are serving you.

Second, you are changing. Visiting homeless people in jail will put fire in your belly.

20. Volunteer in a day shelter for children

Background

When you take part in a day shelter of any kind, you learn some things about life for people without roofs that might not occur to you. Where do poor people go during the day if they have no employment or have to care for children? You'll learn about the policies of your local library (a warm place with bathrooms—but don't get caught sleeping). You'll learn why the stairwells of parking garages smell of urine; there is a surprising dearth of public toilets available to people without a clear reason to be someplace.

How to Do It

This is fairly easy if you're a woman. But if you're a man, you'll likely make the women in the shelters nervous and arouse the suspicion of the regular workers. (Many sheltered women have been abused by men from early in their lives.) Still, it's worth a try.

Use your contacts from other shelters to meet the administrators of the day shelters, getting their help in explaining that you're there to learn parts of the scene that your other projects and friendships have not exposed you to. Shelters often have boards of directors, some of whose members can introduce you as well. It won't take long to build trust. Then you really will learn some things.

21. *Walk through the process of accessing health care with a street person*

Background

Politicians who are critical of welfare expenditures love to make the point that a recipient's income rises far above the poverty line when you factor in the benefit of food stamps and Medicaid. Your explorations will indeed show you heart-warming examples of heroic medical services rendered to street people. It is not too unusual to meet street people who have had hips replaced or other wonderful surgical procedures performed. Prenatal care is available for many expectant mothers without the resources to pay.

To balance this cheering picture, though, walk through the process of applying for these services with a street person. You will make some discoveries about why street people differ from you in your approaches to clock time. To someone who can make an appointment with a dentist that will be kept to the minute and be finished in less than an hour, such a venture can be maddening. What would it take for you to get numb to the frustration that builds up in you during this trip with your friend?

Does this venture make any practical difference to the

homeless person you accompany? Yes, it makes two differences to her and one to you. It encourages her to be accompanied. It may also speed her reception to have somebody who looks like you obviously in her company, taking an interest. And it will change your outlook on things for a long time.

How to Do It

Here again it's necessary to know some street people personally. Explain your interest in learning about the systems that serve them, and ask to accompany them when they next attempt to receive medical care. If they have no immediate need, they will be able to introduce you to somebody who does. And by the end of the expedition, you and your new acquaintance will be firm friends.

Your task is simply to accompany the other person through the system. Dress normally for this experiment. But use public transport—do not offer rides in your car this time—so you can get the feel.

Plan to spend the entire day on a routine visit to the public clinic or hospital.

Some questions may occur to you during the day. Obviously, your impatience will kick loose several: Will they never come back out? How long can this take? But deeper questions may strike you as well. For example, could you keep your job if you had to take off a whole day every time you went to the doctor or dentist? Or what is the real cost to the patient of a visit that consumes an entire day? In what sense is any of this "free" to the recipient?

Learning to keep punctual appointments is important for people reentering the economy. There is simply no way around that unless you're very rich or very poor. But a day or so spent with homeless people trying to access health care may temper your impatience with their casual attitude toward time.

22. Walk through an application for food stamps with a homeless person

Background

Expect this experiment to feel something like the day(s) you spent seeking medical care with a homeless friend. That is, you will encounter the same frustrations with time delays, transportation, and what to do with restless small children, to name a few.

In trying to get food stamps, you may notice a difference. The medical care delivery system you experienced was largely designed by medical people to whom legislators tend to defer when it comes to guidelines. That's probably why it works as well as it does.

But trying to get a welfare service like food stamps is another matter entirely. The public servants have to administer a care delivery system that they had no part in designing. To the contrary, the system they administer has been a political football, a topic of public debate, and a budgetary headache. After all, a widespread belief is that street people do not vote. Who is going to keep their needs in the public budget in a lean year? Also, there will be nit-picking strictures that were godsends on the legislative floor but are nightmarish to administer, that embarrass the civil servants who have to heed them and explain them to clients.

How to Do It

Consider dressing down, and contrast your experience with the one you had accessing health care. Proper identification is always a nuisance—indeed closer to life and death than a mere nuisance. Your friend may not have a driver's license. Official state-issued ID's are obtainable, but that takes at least one lengthy visit to another office. Many welfare programs require a permanent address (though this may not be legal) since their requirements date back before homelessness became so widespread in this country. Some shelters will not permit their addresses to be given as residences, though most will. You and your friend may be able to locate a local church that will permit its address to serve.

Otherwise, the how-to-do-it procedure is similar to going to the hospital or the clinic with a homeless friend.

All sorts of ways to streamline the system will occur to you after only one such foray. Don't waste your time telling the public servants who administer the programs. If they could they would, believe them. No, streamlining these systems, making them humane, will require efforts we'll take up shortly. You will want to join with others in coalitions.

Take some time to reflect on your personal experience on this walk-through. Are you angry? Yet, your friend may not seem angry, merely sort of apathetic, right? Psychologists tell us that anger we can't vent soon sours into depression and then curdles into apathy. Can you feel it? What it feels like to try to improve your condition (or your children's) when your internal weather was that dark?

23. Attend a city council meeting when issues pertaining to homelessness are to be discussed

Background

The city council, like the state legislature, was designed to serve people like you. You belong there as far as the council members are concerned. You pay taxes; you vote; you talk to your neighbors.

Governing bodies are less clear about their duty to poor and homeless people. They don't think that homeless people vote. Homeless people consume taxes rather than pay them, don't they? Their political opinions are not widely sought.

So, when a resolution is brought requesting the opening of a shelter or the licensing of a church to operate a day-care center for poverty-stricken mothers, what considerations will govern the discussion?

Right. They want to know which voting taxpayers will be annoyed with them if the facilities are located in an otherwise convenient (for homeless people) location. Considerations of

making various commercial districts attractive will lead to lo-
cating shelters far from convenient bus lines or grocery stores.

You will soon learn the acronym NIMBY—Not In My Back
Yard. In politics it's sometimes called favoring the church but
opposing the site.

How to Do It

This is where you come in. You ask to speak to the matter,
stating your name, address, occupation (and political party if
it coincides with that of the majority of council members).

By now, you will know a lot more about these issues than
virtually anyone present.

Remember, doing politics takes as much time as applying
for welfare. You may lose again and again in such meetings.
But if you keep your head, remain friendly even when dis-
agreeing, and use reliable information, you will eventually be
welcomed as a resource by the council. And in the give-and-
take of practical politics, you will find that much can be done.

24. Attend a shelter discussion at some neighborhood association

Background

These association meetings are trickier than council meetings, especially if it's not your neighborhood. An elected public servant may manifest some spirit of service. But now you are among worried property owners who believe that their property values will plummet if the poor are allowed to enter their neighborhood. They are not there to represent anybody. They are there to protect their investments. Can you accomplish anything? The answer is a firm, resolute maybe. No, if it's not your neighborhood—though you'll learn a lot. Yes, if it is your neighborhood.

How to Do It

People who live in various localities and want to open them to homeless people have successfully tried several tactics.

First, make sure your information is current, complete, and reliable. It would help, for example, to be able to cite the experience of other neighborhoods that have been hospitable to homeless people without any decline in property values. Local coalition people can obtain this information for you. Essentially, the British council house idea works well in this country, too. That is, a few public units sprinkled into higher income neighborhoods work out to everyone's advantage.

Second, bring with you some of the most attractive and articulate of your friends from the affected population and be their gatekeeper into the discussion. Even scared property owners are human and may respond to real persons.

Third, there have been fascinating applications of drama in these circumstances in various cities. For example, you may favor the opening of a personal care home for deinstitutionalized mental patients in a neighborhood. Naturally, the neighborhood association is against the very thought. So, a group of theater people help some deinstitutionalized people write and produce a play about their lives and circumstances. The play is enacted at the neighborhood meeting, changing the tenor of the gathering—and possibly the outcome.

Perhaps music or other art forms—such as crafts or painting—could be employed if a play is beyond the scope of your group's talents. But drama works well.

25. Learn how your local economy works

Background

Notice that these suggestions are moving in the direction of what is called advocacy, representing the requirements of homeless people in different political and economic arenas. They are also moving toward collaboration with fellow workers.

Moving into advocacy, you will find that much can be done without political (read, slow) efforts. As noted elsewhere, poverty is expensive. It drags down the economy. Whatever improves the lot of the poor will benefit the rich. (Funny how slow we are to realize that; we've believed it the other way around for a long time.) Economic leaders should be approached on behalf of homeless people. They have a natural stake in the prosperity of the formerly poor since that translates into more customers. Prosperity results from consumption. If the poor could consume, we'd all prosper.

You may also be prepared to discover wellsprings of religious charity among economic leaders. Many search for ways to place their occupations at the service of some greater good than simple profit for its own sake. It is often said that greed is the emotional impulse underlying capitalism. But perhaps it would be more true to assert that a combination of delight in taking risks and pride in keeping trust underlies our economic system.

Do not assume you will be brushed off if you approach businesspeople with ideas about how homeless people can have a stake in the economy.

How to Do It

The procedure is roughly like political lobbying. The most important thing to recall in addressing businesspersons is that they routinely make professional use of information and analysis. If they weren't good at both, you wouldn't be talking to them. You need to be prepared to make sense. Be clear about what you know, what you don't know, what it all means.

Learn what you can about the economy of your region. For example, which industries support the local economy? Which ones have withdrawn recently? Which ones are considering coming in? Which ones produce the most jobs? Businesspeople tend to enjoy filling in interested people on such topics. People enjoy talking about what they do and why they do it. Businesspeople are no exception.

Be sure to talk to several because opinions on economics vary. It has been said that if all the nation's economists were laid on the ground head to heel, they would not reach a conclusion; indeed they would point in all directions. (Or did you hear the one about the economics professor who never changed his final exam? He changed only the answers.)

Happily, you are not preparing for an economics final. You are attempting to get some sense of where the local money comes from and where it goes and at what velocity. As you think and talk about these issues and keep your friends on the street at the forefront of your mind, the human community begins to pull back together. Plant ideas about a housing market being out there if somebody knew how to get it developed. At its finest, our economic system is based on mutual advantage. Get that discussion going everywhere you can. Try it.

26. Support your local police

<u>**Background**</u>

Though the life of the police officer on the beat is complicated by the presence of the homeless people who wander his streets, that officer is wonderfully placed to assist homeless people and to help maintain their dignity and safety and their place in the fragile human community. Every effort should be made to support and encourage the police in their endeavors on behalf of homeless people.

In at least one city, some shelter operators kept their ears open around their guests and heard appreciative references to two police officers whose beat was the central city park. To honor the officers, they planned a dinner to which many homeless people, the officers' superiors, and the press were invited. You can guess the immediate impact that one dinner had on police attitudes toward homeless people. That awards dinner for deserving police officers is now a yearly event.

Police officers have a difficult time in our society. As a population, they tend to be men and women with a deep sense of justice and personal duty and a wish to be of service. They believe in the law. You are more likely to hear a discussion of justice in the abstract among police officers (provided you get close enough to overhear their conversation) than you will ever hear among attorneys. Yet, they regularly encounter resentment and bitterness from the public they serve.

The police in many localities provide generous service to homeless people, taking them to shelters when it gets cold, responding to their crises of health or property, often extending leniency in the enforcement of laws that hassle the poor. When orders "come down" from some official that the homeless are to be swept from the downtown area in response to some publicity-fraught activity, the police often respond with embarrassed reluctance. They know it isn't fair.

So why do the police get such bad mention from people who regularly work with homeless folks?

Consider two reasons. First, as noted above, often instructions have "come down" that the homeless people are to be rousted for some purpose or other. Although the initiative normally comes from local merchants through the mayor to the police chief, the actual job is up to the police officer on the beat, who has to absorb the resentment.

Second, when you track down specific episodes of harassment of homeless people by "the police," the culprits often turn out to be private security guards, not sworn peace officers. Security guards, though heavily armed, are usually poorly trained and have no charter to assist the public. They work for the man who owns the building, and if he says, "Keep those bums off my lawn," or "Get that scum off my steps," there's no percentage in a security guard's being gentle about it.

How to Do It

This project will take collaborative effort.

Convince your civic club, your religious congregation, your corporation, or a group of friends to offer regular appreciative awards to police officers who exhibit conspicuous kindness to street people.

Get some of your new friends who are homeless (or other people who serve with them) to let you know when particular officers treat them kindly. Again, listen for *stories*.

Hold a banquet in the officers' honor, making sure their superiors know that an award is to be granted. Give the press plenty of notice; see to it that the paper and the evening TV news cover the event.

You will be surprised at the good this project will do your homeless friends—let alone your police department.

27. Learn how municipal and state politics work

Background

Studies indicate that you have to live in a neighborhood at least five years before you exhibit any interest at all in local government. It would be nice if you had a similar five-year immunity to their decisions, wouldn't it? Dream on.

If you want good government, be it.

Government was not designed for poor people. Even the United States Constitution assumed that a voter was a property owner; a slave, as you recall, counted only as a fraction of a human being for the purpose of a census. Amendment XIV remedied this injustice. Government is for people who pay taxes and vote. Government is enthusiastically for people who finance political campaigns and display a sensitive understanding of the fact that people do not contribute to politicians merely as a hobby.

Once you get involved with homeless people, you become aware that private charity is not the answer to this problem. First, the scale of the problem is too great. Second, legislation is needed to protect poor people from various forms of exploitation. Third, tax incentives are needed to encourage investments that will benefit the poor. All that requires government efforts.

Our public discussion of governmental responsibility for the protection of the poor is polluted with nonsense. We hear it said that such concern is the job of the private sector, volunteers, and the church and synagogue. That is a way of saying we don't take the plight of poor people seriously. Imagine entrusting our national defense to a volunteer militia. Or the gathering of taxes to freewill gifts. Or police and fire services to local businesspeople. Poverty is as big a problem as Moammar Khadafy, Saddam Hussein, crime, fire, or tax evasion.

In the Hebrew Scriptures (the Christian Old Testament) the obligation to care for the poor was laid as heavily on the king and judge as on the priest, prophet, or private citizen. It follows theologically that in a secular state in which church and state are separated, both share the responsibility for caring for God's poor.

So, if poor people and homeless people are to participate in the life of the community, local and state government must take an interest. It will be up to people like you to insist that those forms of government serve all the citizens. And to do so, you have to understand government.

How to Do It

Divide your research into three piles, naming them *What, How,* and *Who.*

What: Learn what offices are in local government. A call to the information number in your municipal, county, and state phone listings will get you plenty of information in the mail, lots of it free.

How: Learn which offices are responsible for specific

tasks. Learn how budgets are formed, spent, and supervised. Learn how a bill originates, where it has to go to be passed, and so forth.

Who: Learn who holds key positions. Learn their party affiliations. Discover their interests and commitments.

Be careful at this juncture not to seem shrill. More than one activist has achieved such notoriety that she has merely to enter a legislative hearing room for all eyes to roll up into people's heads as they brace themselves against her blast, snickering behind their hands. Do not copy such activists.

A group that takes this suggestion up as a project can get it done even more quickly. Once you set about this, you will be surprised how much you know in so little time. With this research under way, ways will emerge so that you can get local government to serve homeless people. The very process of gathering all that information will announce to people in government that taxpayers are taking an interest in their interest in the poor. As will be noted in the next suggestion, some politicians will actually welcome your concern.

28. Befriend your local politician

It's time to put some faces and voices to the names you have accumulated. You have learned a bit about who's who in local and state government. You have been considering the thought that these people serve *you* and people like you. It's time to test that. It's time to get to know some of them personally.

This is going to be fun and interesting. Forget all the caricatures about nasty, overweight pols dividing the spoils in rooms choked with cigar smoke. The folks you're going to meet make a living by meeting the public and charming them. You are the public, and you are about to be charmed.

Legislators, senators, and council members get their positions by having a passionate interest in something that they are able to sell to the active populace, those who actually turn out to vote. Politicians are alert activists. They tend to be extroverts. They manifest considerable personal force in conversation. All of that can make for a discussion you'll remember long after it's over.

The effective ones (and you will find many) are only too aware of the complexity of our society, the conflict of values equally good, the relentless requirement that legislation make midcourse corrections in the way society is going, and the hopeless impossibility of a single politician's having enough information on any single issue (let alone a welter of issues) to be able to take and defend a position that is recognizably wise.

That's where you come in. Make no mistake about how necessary you are. You represent an *informed* interest in an urgent issue: the plight of homeless people. You are information. Your private interest in homeless people makes you a potential honorary staff member for every politician you take the trouble to address. And if the politician you discuss these matters with finds your information reliable (and your personal manner not too abrasive), you will become a trusted resource.

In this way, over time, you can accomplish a lot for homeless people.

How to Do It

First, find out who your local representatives are by name, home address, phone number, and working office in the district. Get this information on your municipal or county councillors, state legislators, and state senator. Chances are, you already know who your federal congressman and senators are, but you may not know their local office numbers.

Next, make an appointment with each one for conversation. Some may wish to take you to lunch. Express your interest in the condition of people without homes. Ask their perspective on these matters. Offer to supply them with information, stories (always stories), and considerations as they come your way. Show a genuine interest in anything they want to talk to you about because they may wish to sample your opinion on some unrelated issue; that's fair, after all.

Now, make sure that you keep feeding information to your representatives. Stay on the alert for bills coming up that affect poor people, and provide relevant material to them in time for use. As an individual, you won't be able to track most of the bills, but as you get better at it, you'll find yourself gravitating to a primary area of interest (e.g., mental health issues, physical health, housing, civil rights, etc.). You will develop buddies in related areas, leading to fruitful and sometimes merry collaborations.

Be certain that your information is accurate. If your representative embarrasses herself using information you supplied, your lobbying days are over. But every time information you supply proves useful, you are deeper into the system.

Stay courteous. The out-front manner of your representative protects a core as sensitive as your own. If politicians learn to expect you to be abrasive, sarcastic, or shrill, you will instantly acquire an undesirable nickname in the privacy of their offices.

29. Get to know public officials in relevant departments

Background

This activity is similar to the previous one—and fraught with happy surprises as well. You can get to know all sorts of public employees whose daily work affects poor people.

As you start getting to know these people, you will make three discoveries. First, you will discover pockets of startling competence and deep concern. These people care about what they do. Because they care, your interest will be welcome. So don't be shy.

Second, these folks are frustrated by the limits they must operate within. Most of them wish they had more money, more help, more time, and more energy to devote to their clients. You may well come away from a meeting with a sense that you and your friends can achieve things in some areas that public officials cannot.

Third, you will discover that these people can be of great help in pointing you toward the right politicians, armed with the right information. In many state or local administrations, people at this level are not permitted to lobby for their own areas. But if they trust you, they can wind you up, point you right, and switch you on. Everybody wins when you take part in such projects. The bureaucrats get another pipeline into their elected bosses' attention field; the politicians get reliable information that won't blow up in their faces; the homeless people get more accurately targeted assistance.

How to Do It

Begin by talking to people who provide care and services for homeless people. Ask them who they deal with on a municipal, county, or state level. Then call those people and ask for appointments. The agenda for the first meeting will include declaring your interest in homeless people and getting informed about how this person experiences the issues related to homeless people. Expect the meetings to go overtime. Bureaucrats need love, too, and they enjoy having people take an interest.

Find out who prepares the budgets for the various levels of government to pass each year. These are often key people to encourage when some project you're aware of will benefit from public funding.

30. Communicate often

Background

Democracy for the most part works. Elected representatives really represent; that is, they represent the people they hear from. No matter how good an idea may be, people have to be out there saying they're for it before representatives go into action.

Most people never think about that. We congratulate ourselves on being a free country every time we have an election. In fact, every time a bill or a resolution comes up for consideration, the public has another election. But this ballot is in the form of letters, petitions, and phone calls. Do you vote in these ways? This form of citizenship is as important as voting for candidates and is the logical next step after electing officials.

You had better believe that somebody in your politicians' offices reads the mail—at least someone weighs it. They expect to hear from their people.

This is where your visits to these folks are going to pay off. If in your letter you refer to the pleasure you took in your recent lunch together, the secretary who reads the representative's mail for her will put it on her desk in case "this one" requires a personal response.

How to Do It

Come on. Just do it. It's so easy to do, almost as easy as it is to overlook.

Write or call whenever you know your representatives face a vote on something that affects poor people. Write to insist that they help keep some project in the budget, mentioning the name or number of the item if you can learn it.

If you are entitled to use a formal letterhead, do so. If you can get your letter typed (with some of those "GT/nal" codes in the lower left-hand corner), your elected reader can see that you paid somebody to produce the letter.

By now, you should have amassed some friends who share your interest. They may lack your passion, your activism, or your civic guts, but you can enlist them to write letters to their representatives without much trouble. Ask them to use their letterheads, too. The more letters, the better.

Warning: Avoid word-for-word duplicate letters over several signatures. It works better if each letter is personally drafted. The rule is that one personal visit is worth fifty letters or one hundred phone calls.

That's democracy. Really.

31. Start reflecting on your experiences so far, looking for stereotypes

Background

A stereotypical notion of a group of people is a dishonest way of "knowing." "Knowing" is put in quotes because the stereotype only pretends to be knowledge. But that "knowledge" will often not survive scrutiny. Stereotyping is dishonest because it allows us to avoid some less desirable emotional reaction, such as fear, envy, self-criticism, or sympathy.

By now, your efforts with homeless people should be having at least two noticeable effects on you. First, as your social horizons have expanded to include all kinds of people whom you would never have thought of as acquaintances—let alone friends—your emotional courage has grown to keep up. Fear of other races is drying up in the face of the many actual experiences you are amassing while you are becoming a more accurate guidance system by teaching what districts a wise person really will avoid at certain times of the day or night. Envy is disappearing as you learn to delight in particular friends whose charming embodiment of various enviable traits makes those traits available to you. Self-criticism now seems to be an emotional racket of the uninvolved—a population that no longer includes you. And free-floating sympathy is getting more specific as you appreciate the options that your friends still possess.

Second, your experience so far has supplied you with real data, all the actual stories you have accumulated. You have spent hours with people as clever as yourself; those occasions temper any notions of significant difference in intellectual ability. So you speak some French or Spanish and have been to Europe, Hawaii, or Disney World? Your friends on the streets know some dialects of English that they had to learn a lot faster than you learned yours and have been some places that are strange to you—and you know it. You now have a more realistic knowledge of how honesty works on the street in matters of money, property, and living space—knowledge that lets you spot disparaging remarks at suburban parties as far too simplistic.

This suggestion works for groups other than minority groups or categories of poor people.

Prepare to be surprised by feelings of sadness as you do this one, a nostalgic longing for a previous time when things seemed simple. Your experience is teaching you to quit judging and to start understanding. Judging is a whole lot easier on the mind and heart than understanding is. If understanding were as easy as judging, a lot more wisdom would be apparent in our public life.

Some people think that the human mind cannot judge and understand simultaneously. When you make a judgment about something or somebody, your understanding has hit its ceiling; it can go no higher. When you understand something or somebody, your impulse to judge recedes noticeably.

For all of the difficulty and sadness, though, people who know the difference would rather be wise than judgmental.

There is no getting around the reality that the public deals with complex social problems by self-serving, judgmental oversimplifications. We conjure reality with stereotypes. If only the landlords would lower their rates, if only social workers wouldn't try to build self-protecting empires, if only politicians weren't on the take. . . . You've heard it all. But it's no longer that simple for you, right? Now we're talking about people you know.

As you do this exercise, resist any temptation to despair. Remember, there are no simple solutions to simple problems, but there are complex solutions to complex problems. So let's wade deeper into the complexity.

You are ready to examine your remaining stereotypes. That project will make you an even more serviceable citizen. Why is that practical? How does it help a homeless person? It helps by seeding our populace with men and women who can raise the level of our public discussion on matters of poverty. Our nation can think when asked to think. We must ask. The (slow) result will be more responsible journalism, more accurate legislation, and more adventurous commerce. Anything that promotes those things helps the poor and constitutes a civic duty.

How to Do It

Take a pad of paper or a notebook. (This is good work for your journal if you have been keeping one.) Across the top of the page, list the different racial groups you have had dealings with. Do not omit your own! It might look something like this:

Black   White   Hispanic   Native American

Under each group, list typical stereotypes you're used to associating with that group. (I would supply a model for you, but you get the idea; besides, I don't want somebody casually browsing through this book to fasten down on it.)

List other types of people horizontally across the top of a page, such as the following, and again list stereotypes:

politicians	*politicians*	*social workers*	*businesspersons*
(local)	(state)		

You will probably need more than one sheet. Or maybe you can turn the sheet sideways.

Now go through the list several times, making the following notations.

First, check the ones you formerly agreed with.

Next, mark the ones that are clearly contradicted by your actual experiences with your friends.

Next, sketch in what you understand may account for a given stereotype (e.g., for *unpunctual* you might write in, "These people experience time as their enemy, something to 'kill' rather than to schedule").

Survey the results. Have you changed your opinions to any extent since you began these projects?

It's more complex than it used to be, right? But take heart. The more complex a system is, the more vulnerable it is to change. You may already have changed it to some extent by your involvements so far.

32. Get more for your money

Background

Charities vary in the percentage of money raised that actually gets to the target group. This percentage is unstable; without steady self-examination, any charity will tend to bureaucratize with more money going to administration and less to service. The reason for that tendency is that service providers burn out before their contracts expire. So they redefine their duties, in some cases actually multiplying the paperwork they complain about since it affords relief from the emotional fatigue of intractable poverty. (Street people call this tendency spin, and people who so redefine their duties are called spin doctors.) As much as we might sympathize with their plights when we view them in that light (more than one reader may recognize spinning from settings closer to home), we want the money we give to poor people actually to reach poor people in some way.

How to Do It

Before giving money to a charity, ascertain the percentage of your gift that will go to overhead. Anything under 15 percent is considered decent. Unless you want to inject the money directly into the situation (and that's not wise for a beginner), you owe the service providers some overhead for doing your work for you until you learn how. A charitable organization is supposed to tell you that percentage on inquiry. It's the law. Don't be afraid to ask.

Consider whether you want this to be a seasonal effort or year-round. Many readers will choose a charity that serves meals all year instead of a single Thanksgiving meal or a Christmas stocking fund.

Do not be deterred by the small amount you may have to give. Many worthwhile efforts subsist miraculously on many small gifts that arrive just in time when needed. (Get the persons involved to tell you some of their stories.)

The ideal service to poor people is personal service combined with financial contributions to professionals who are doing a good job. But either effort or money is preferable to neither.

33. Start inserting your knowledge into discussions of homelessness

Background

Words are thought—or its absence—so calling things by the right name is a civic duty. You have probably noticed that this discussion rarely employs the word *homeless* as a noun; we speak instead of *homeless people*. Homelessness is a problem, but homeless people are not. As noted previously, not much wisdom is apparent in our public discourse these days, especially on highly charged issues such as poverty where everybody has several self-protective opinions. It's up to you to inject some wisdom from time to time if you expect to live in a society that values it.

You should heed some principles if you're not going to get the reputation of the world's leading expert, one who can empty a party by simply arriving.

- People don't like being lectured to.
- People don't like being made to look bad.
- People don't like to feel guilty.

- People like to figure things out themselves so as to feel smart.
- It is always an advantage to seem less wise than you really are.

That brief list may appear daunting. But concocting conversational strategies and tactics based on it really is possible.

Perhaps the most difficult principle to heed is the last one, the one about its being to your advantage that people don't know how smart you really are. In discussing the plight of homeless people, that means you don't talk much about what you're doing downtown and you don't let it be known that you possess some expertise on this topic, that you may be the only one in the present circle entitled to an opinion. Until the grace and charity of that stance make it habitual, you can cultivate it by treating yourself to the delight of possessing a secret life. Be sure to play it innocently—no smirks of secret knowledge, no lifted eyebrows, no curling the mustache (if you're a man) or playing with your hair with your fingers and a flounce of the head (if you're a woman).

How to Do It

In conversations that turn to matters of homelessness and poverty, welfare, or taxes, confine your participation to asking questions. That stratagem fulfills all five principles listed above.

- You are obviously not lecturing when you ask for more information or alternative explanations.
- You can phrase a question innocently to avoid making it an accusation, so the others don't feel bad exploring it.
- Questions invite people more deeply into the complexity of these matters than guilt allows them.

- Questions allow people to display their cleverness; that's why people do crossword puzzles, after all.
- Questions (unless you're Socrates) don't make it plain that you know the answer and others don't.

Finally, questions linger in the mind long after statements have been forgotten. (That's why Jesus preferred questions to lectures.) A lingering question that won't let you go finally disrupts your previous frame of reference. Like an oyster making a pearl from sandy irritations, your mind makes new insights from nagging questions.

That's not as swaggering a social posture as being the only one in the gathering who knows all the baseball statistics back to Abner Doubleday or all the episodes on last week's soaps, but it is a cultivatable taste nonetheless. Some of us prefer it.

What *do* you ask people? Leaving the specific formulation of questions up to you, the general answer is, you ask people questions that lead them into deeper water. Questions like, "Have you ever known anyone who was actually homeless?" can cancel judgmental generalizations. (Do not ask something like, "How many homeless people do you actually know in person?" That's not a question; it's an accusation that leaves the other person embarrassed and annoyed.) You want your line of questioning to disrupt previous clarity, to seek exceptions to stereotypes, to find multiple causes.

The fruit of that social posture is wisdom, however slow to develop.

34. Pay your child support promptly to your ex-wife

Background

Well, okay. You're not divorced. You're still single. You're not even a guy; you're a *woman*, for crying out loud. Still, do you get the point? By now, you have connected with some women with children in shelters who are not all that different from you. Every now and then you meet the former wife of a physician in a shelter.

No-fault divorce has produced an effect nobody intended: the feminization of poverty.

Think of the woman in our society reared with the expectation that her life script could and would be satisfied by finding some promising male and linking her fortunes to his productive capabilities. That his loyalties would accompany his productivity was a truth too obvious to question.

As serviceable as that scenario may once have been, as desirable as it might remain for many women, it nevertheless contains at least three flaws.

First, many women are no longer content with domestic roles that permit no cultivation of their other talents, strengths, or interests. The campaigns these women have mounted to legitimize alternative roles have changed the social schema for all of us. (This matter is far too complex for us to judge it good or bad; trying to understand it is preferable.) Being a housewife is no longer the obvious career option it once was for many women. Its dignity has suffered, and with its dignity its entitlement to special consideration. Alimony is no longer so automatic when couples divorce.

Second, the industrial and service economies no longer pay one worker a family wage. For a couple to own a home, possess cars for each driver, take vacation trips, and exchange memorable presents during holiday seasons, both parties must have paying jobs. Yet, wages reflect the old assumption that a working woman is only supplementing her husband's income (and is entitled to his health benefits). Women are not paid as much as men in equivalent jobs. No persons (except those in the upper and upper middle classes) have as much money today as they would have had thirty years ago. Prices for food, rent, and transportation have risen faster than wages have. A divorced mother is in deeper trouble today than ever—as is a divorced husband with child support payments.

Third (and most embarrassing for a male to discuss in print), the cultural climate today diminishes a man's sense of responsibility for his family. Shrill voices he vaguely associates with women's liberation contribute to his sense of guilt when he thinks of his wife and family; consequently, he thinks of them less often. And the men's magazines he reads in his barbershop (as well as the ads he reads and sees everywhere) suggest that he ought to be having a more libidinous time of it, that he should be living it up. Both forces diminish his eagerness to make his payments after he divorces.

The result? As the divorce rate rises, expect to see more and more women of your class in serious financial trouble. And these days the final safety net is a charity shelter.

How to Do It

First, like I said, if you're a divorced guy, make your payments and make them on time.

Second, if you're an industrialist, see what you and your peers can do to get wages up and costs down.

Third, quit reading soft-porn magazines and life-style advertisements. They feed poverty, believe it or not. They distort reality and leach away your sense of responsibility for other people. They make you feel *entitled* to luxuries that feed your addiction to possessions whose price would better serve your homeless friends.

Fourth, and most likely, do everything you can in your social circle to promote the stability of marriage. Marital instability feeds social instability—ultimately feeding poverty as the human community deteriorates.

That will take courage. In these days of mobility when we are temporary residents wherever we live, our tendency is not to meddle in the privacy of other people. When a couple you've met are said to be having trouble, your tendency will be to pull back to give them space. It's important to see that pullback as part of the same deterioration of human community that permits homelessness. So wade into it with the same courage you've been showing in the shelters and food lines. Do everything you can to promote sensible reflection on the part of both individuals. Enlist divorced people to tell them what it's really like. Share the name of a counselor you trust.

Most important, enrich, stabilize, and enjoy your own marriage. People need to know it can be done.

Consider the fact that your own rich marriage is the best platform from which to mount efforts on behalf of homeless people. You need someplace nourishing to come home to.

35. Encourage the police's efforts to control illegal drugs

Background

Please notice that the drugs need controlling. It may seem easier to control drug users. But the only effective police efforts against drug abuse will prove those that cut off the supply rather than punish the users.

Though as of this writing there is some evidence that the middle and upper classes in America are tapering off somewhat in their use of harmful substances—cocaine, tobacco, alcohol—the underclass keeps those industries working nights. Because their use of illegal substances remains high—and because members of the underclass are, after all, not big-time voters or taxpayers—public discussion flirts with the idea of simply decriminalizing narcotics.

That would, according to some people, save the police time and money presently frittered away in a losing battle against a victimless crime; it would deprive the criminal establishment that traffics in the stuff of its major income; and it would provide the public with an additional source of revenues.

Those are attractive benefits. But the real cost remains far too high. The fact is, cocaine and its crack derivative cripple their users. A grim joke describes cocaine as nature's way of telling you you've got too much money. You don't have your money long—or your house, your car, or your family—once you start using. Street people who get into crack will tell you that if you start to use crack today, in six months you will have fallen from your middle-class eminence to the shelters, shanties, overpasses, heating grates, and doorways. For most people, once is all it takes. Homeless people are already most at risk because they have so little else going for them.

Suppose we did decriminalize the use of crack. We would still guarantee a constant supply of crackheads on foot and in cars. Do you want to be out there with them? And, most unethically, we would condemn the users to a short life at a miserable level of social and economic existence. Crime would remain a major source for the fees, even if the outlets were legal, because crackheads would have few alternatives after rendering themselves incapable of sustained effort at lucrative tasks.

As long as we tolerate cocaine and crack on our streets, we perpetuate an underclass into which the helpless will fall.

If we can dry up the supply—as many cities have succeeded in doing with heroin—some of the present addicts can recover. People recover from addictions if they can't get their fix. Furthermore, the existing poor will not have their economic recuperative abilities leached away into an expensive pseudonirvana.

How to Do It

Use your contacts in city hall and on the police force to see legalization campaigns coming, and call upon everything you've learned about grass-roots politics to forestall them.

As with the programs of awards for police officers who assist homeless people, see that officers who rack up good records in the war on drugs get public recognition. These officers deserve our gratitude. It's hard to imagine what a fair wage would be for people who engage in that struggle, so the very least that we can do is to guarantee them a rich emotional income for their pains and risks.

Officers get killed fighting drug traffickers. Citizens' groups must take an active interest in the care of their families by such projects as supporting their education, arranging scholarships, and the like. Those actions let other officers know that we all value their work.

36. Build a house: help Habitat for Humanity and similar organizations

Background

Today several charitable groups around the country are building houses for poor and homeless people on a turnkey, sweat-equity basis. That means these groups buy building lots with charitable donations, use materials that are largely donated, hire a foreman and specialists (plumbers, electricians, etc.), and build family dwellings using labor from volunteer groups and from the beneficiaries themselves. The new owners make the mortgage payments back to the charity—usually at an affordable rate, perhaps $175 per month. When the payments are complete (say, within ten years), the family owns the house free and clear. The payments go back into a revolving fund for the purchase of new land and materials for additional houses.

In this way, whole neighborhoods are being healthily infiltrated with highly motivated poor people who are back in the economy and intend to stay there. Inserting such housed families stabilizes neighborhoods that had been run down without displacing lower income people. Offering turnkey, sweat-equity housing cleans up neighborhoods without yuppifying them.

The best known group of this nature is Habitat for Humanity, an outgrowth of Clarence Jordan's Koinonia Farms commune near Americus, Georgia. Most large cities have a Habitat number in the phone directory.

There is much to commend this procedure. It gets deserving people off the streets and into houses in which they build equity. It populates neighborhoods with people who know that they are citizens. It is one of the best uses of charity dollars going because the money you donate keeps working. Building houses is enormous fun. Even more fun is working alongside a previously disadvantaged family that will be moving in. The whole project in all of its aspects constitutes restoration of the human community.

How to Do It

If you are seeking a good cause to contribute money to, simply call Habitat or look for one of their ads in the paper. There may be similar groups in your vicinity you will want to support.

Consider asking your civic club or religious congregation to take on a house as a project. A single group can build a single house or may collaborate with other groups.

Building a house activates young people. Take your children or the children of friends with you. They will find it life changing.

These organizations will rush a speaker to your group if you request one for a program. Nothing succeeds like success, and these groups have a great success record. People who had felt that any efforts to assist homeless people would be futile readily take heart when they have this procedure explained to them.

This will be a fruitful investment of your time and your money. Once a group builds a house with a poor family, the members will want to build another and another and another.

37. Consider joining a religious congregation

Background

What does joining a religious congregation have to do with helping homeless people? Well, consider four reasons for becoming religiously involved as part of your activities with homeless people.

First, religious congregations are already carrying the bulk of the weight in caring for homeless people. In synagogues and churches people get motivated for this sort of service. It probably has something to do with the fact that the Hebrew and Christian Scriptures are socially revolutionary; you can't hang around where they are read without being activated to some extent. Becoming active in a congregation is a way of getting with a group bound to contain some folks who share your interests.

Making a connection with a religious congregation is a good first step in getting with coalitions for efforts that require a group of people, such as lobbying, letter writing, home building, opening shelters and kitchens, and so forth.

Second, you may have recognized that many of your street

friends are religious. With their backs to the wall, they learn to pray. They may be a bit shy talking to you about their religious faith. But if you're willing to let it be known that religious faith is a value of your own, that forms another plank in the bridge between you.

Third, you're probably more religious than you think anyway. You've read this far in this book, haven't you? That means you have a sense of a broader good. There is some advantage to cultivating that personal value in a setting where others share your interest and to dipping into the centuries-old traditions of men and women who have enriched their lives by devoting them to others. Since the United States is religiously pluralistic, you should have little trouble finding a group whose approach to things is congenial to yours.

Fourth, in a way that nobody can entirely explain, prayer seems to be a really good thing to do. When you lie awake at night thinking about your friends downtown and those who care for them, prayer is a splendid employment for the longings, yearnings, and energies those tossing thoughts kick loose. Being networked with others who are praying for the same thing around the same times is sturdying.

How to Do It

Get out the Yellow Pages and turn to the church and synagogue listings. Start calling the ones that look promising. Ask the person who answers what that congregation has going in outreach programs to poor people and homeless people. You'll be able to tell from the reply if they are the type of congregation you are seeking.

Ask other volunteers downtown where they worship. Chances are, if you like a covolunteer, you'll also like her worshiping community.

Ask your homeless friends where they go to services whenever they go, and offer to accompany them.

Again, considering taking part in a worshiping community is another small contribution to restoring the community at large.

38. Persuade your congregation to offer a day shelter for women and children

Background

The major difference between males without homes and females without homes is the presence or absence of responsibility for children. Men typically don't have small children with them to provide care for. Women typically do.

That works against women economically. Let's say a man gets a minimum wage job. Assuming he is on his own, he can do what he wants with his take-home pay. (Not that he can stretch $610 per month very far, as you will have ascertained, but his situation beats that of his sisters.) A woman working for minimum wage must pay out a hefty portion of it for child care. That reduces the meager amount she has for food and housing.

All that means it's essential that affordable and dependable child care be made available for working women. Not just women in shelters, mind you. All lower income women with children have this pressing need. If reliable and affordable child care is available, many women will not wind up in shelters.

The lack of affordable—and safe—child care for this class of women is a national disgrace. Until the public sector and private industry take up this matter, religious congregations will carry the primary burden. For you to take an interest in this area, you will need to work collaboratively with other motivated people. Your synagogue, church, civic organization, or corporation may take on this project. It's most likely to be a religious group of some kind, however.

How to Do It

In setting up a day-shelter/child-care program, a religious congregation has two advantages.

First, a religious congregation can do almost anything it wants to do with its property if it can show that the program is charitable. It does not have to justify its use of its property to neighborhood groups. If it offers itself as a shelter, it can even in some localities take its time in meeting codes for commercial day-care centers. (Look into this with care, though; this suggestion often only works if you're careful to call it a shelter, not a day-care program.)

Second, such groups are readily organized into volunteer teams. You can get lots of free labor from them.

Depending on the location, the group may have to arrange for some sort of transportation pool if public transportation does not reach it.

Of all the shelter-type activities you can organize out of a religious congregation, a day shelter for children will be the most attractive to the volunteers. People are more likely to volunteer for a children's shelter than they would be for, say, a hospice for people living with AIDS. But remember, you get further understanding some things than you do trying to judge them.

Use energy where you can find it.

39. Consider a regular day-care program for nonhomeless working mothers

Background

Beginning a regular day-care program takes a little more work than offering a day shelter for children. It requires a license, building compliance with various codes, and probably a paid staff.

Although the effort is greater, some conservative congregations prefer this sort of program over a shelter for homeless children. Maybe it seems more legitimate or something, running less risk of attracting undesirable people into the neighborhood.

(Repeat five times, "I would rather understand than judge.")

So why do it? Why kowtow to mere respectability when so many really poor people need your help? Because some of the respectable women who will park their kids at the center are only one or two house payments from the shelters themselves. If you help make it possible for them to remain at work, you keep them housed.

How to Do It

Ask somebody who has done it in a nonprofit day-care program, as in a church. They will have many helpful suggestions to offer based on their experiences.

40. Offer regular transportation to homeless people

Background

By now, your experiences with homeless people have fully acquainted you with what has been called the tyranny of distance. It gets to people all kinds of ways, not all of them obvious. Of course it's a nuisance not to have a car for getting to work, fetching groceries, rushing kids to the doctor's office, and running daily errands. Less apparent is the sense of claustrophobia that builds up in you when you're on foot in a mobile society. That choking sense eventually passes through rage to apathy.

If you spend any time on the street on a "plunge," the resentment you will feel for those who blandly drive past you in their cars will surprise you with its force. So we're not just talking about convenience here. We're talking about mental health and reducing the frustrations that sometimes erupt into lawbreaking.

Public transportation is not always an answer. It is often slow, especially if you have to make transfers. Proximity to bus and subway lines pushes up rents, as you have probably already discovered. So really poor people may live a distance from public lines. Also, it costs a lot of money. A single woman with two children over three years old can pay as much as $420 per month just getting around on public transportation.

In many cities whole districts cannot be reached by public transportation—by insistence of local residents who fear a rise in crime resulting from easier availability to the poor. Ironically, the shops and restaurants in these vicinities have to pay top dollar to their employees because the labor supply is so thin. Persons who need these jobs the most cannot reach them.

How to Do It

Let's assume you don't feel ready yet to start a citywide low-cost taxi service for every street person in town. You can start simply by selecting one or two of your friends who are homeless. Decide before talking to them how much time you can commit per week without its disrupting the rest of your life. It's best if you can select a regular time. Offer that time to them and to another of their friends they choose. You will find that these times become the high point of your week.

Be clear about your limits and boundaries on these errands. If you give yourself permission to be clear and firm about them, you can relax and won't resent them.

Don't expect such a commitment to last as long as a year with any given person. Your friends do not intend to remain on the street. The kind of help you're extending is going to speed their returns to the society of people who have their own housing.

Most public transportation systems offer tokens and weekly and monthly passes. Consider making such passes a gift to your homeless friends. In many cities the cost would be around ten dollars per week, but it's worth much more than that to your friend.

41. Talk to religious landlords about tithing space

Background

As noted any number of times so far, much of the problem of people not having homes could be solved if the supply of affordable housing were to grow. Ultimately, private enterprise will have to figure out how to increase the supply.

A religious congregation offers a natural setting for that sort of discussion. As you may have discovered already, the Hebrew Scriptures (which Christians embrace as well) require that a certain portion of a cultivated field or orchard or vineyard be left unharvested so that orphans and widows may gather sustenance. Surely that principle could apply to housing as well if housing is a commodity that certain people cultivate for profit, that people grow.

How to Do It

In most congregations there are people who have invested in rental real estate. A headache for them is keeping a supply of suitable tenants. Try the following approach.

First, interest them in using a portion of their investment to serve the poor according to biblical principles. Ask the leader of the congregation to agree to receive the rental space as a charitable gift to the congregation.

Second, offer to screen some homeless families for stability, honesty, and suitability as renters. Shelter operators will help you with this so your landlord friends and congregation leaders won't have an unhappy experience.

Third, help your friend arrange an affordable rent rate for the former street family. The head of your congregation will work with you to get the difference between the going rate and the rate offered the street family declared a gift to the congregation; hence, it's deductible.

A lot of housing stands vacant out there. It's good business to have people living in that housing. It's good religion, too.

42. Share clothing

Background

Clothing is plumage. It makes a statement about you from across the street or across the room. It tells the nearsighted what sex you are, how wealthy you are, what class you belong to, how educated you are, how refined, and how hygienic. By the time you open your mouth to speak with a stranger, as many as half of the impressions that person is going to carry about you have already formed.

That truism operates cruelly in the lives of homeless people. No matter how many clothes they formerly possessed, they now have to travel light. When they were put out on the street, scavengers may have taken their belongings off the sidewalk. Access to laundry services for their remaining clothing is restricted. (Forget all about dry cleaning.) Add to that the fact that life on the street changes neck size, waistline, and shoe size. All those factors add up to a street person's making a sartorial statement that will likely make his return to the community of the "roofed" more difficult. On job interviews a poorly dressed person is a loser.

Not all homeless people are comfortable with the notion

of being charity recipients. Simply giving away clothes to somebody can meet with a bittersweet reception.

Consider some alternatives to outright gifts.

How to Do It

First, find a recipient or pipelines to recipients. If the recipient is one of your friends on the street and you or someone in your family is of a similar size, it's fairly simple. Gifts are appropriate among friends. Otherwise, arrange with a shelter director to receive and distribute the clothing you want to give away.

Select the clothing you want to give away. Say to yourself, "I really don't wear that item all that much."

The best way to do it is to save the selection task for a day when you're in a bad mood. If your mood is dark enough, you'll ruthlessly give away quite a lot. Try to be hard on yourself. What proportion of the clothing in your closet do you really care for? The relief you will feel as you rid yourself of each little-used item will surprise you. (Monks and nuns report that it's a real pleasure.)

Now take them to a dry cleaner to be *cleaned* and laundered. Nobody wants unwashed clothes, but the pleasure of getting clothing wrapped in plastic covers is considerable.

If you're making gifts to an individual, offer only one item per wardrobe category—one jacket, one sweater, one pair of shoes, and so on. Too much property is heavy to carry around and difficult to store. Too much stuff makes them vulnerable to predators.

Consider opening a thrift shop out of your congregation or getting your congregation to rent space for such a shop close to the downtown area. A shop space near where homeless people hang out may not be expensive. The advantages to opening a thrift shop include

- preserving the dignity of the recipients by allowing them to buy
- creating a place where you and your friends can meet and befriend homeless people

43. Encourage businesspeople to develop low-cost housing

Background

Some students of homelessness insist that the problem is primarily one of lack of affordable housing. Though others cite additional factors (e.g., deinstitutionalization, crack addiction), there is no question that the lack of affordable housing is a major difficulty. The old-fashioned rooming house is no longer part of our social landscape.

Housing for low-income people seems vulnerable right now. Every time we widen a freeway, build an overpass, erect a stadium, it is likely that we raze housing for low-income people that will not be replaced, certainly not nearby. The urban renewal campaigns in the sixties devastated whole neighborhoods. Our economic and political systems do not presently countenance the government's directly undertaking to house vast segments of the population; yet, they offer few objections to its depriving them of housing.

How to Do It

Start planting the following idea among people you know who own rental properties, who are developers, or who have venture capital to spread around. (Religious congregations and civic groups are fertile ground for such conversations since their members often share social values friendly to assisting poor people.)

The idea is simple supply-and-demand capitalism. The housing crisis among poor people is a demand seeking a supply. Don't let it embarrass you that you don't have a complete design for how the supply can be supplied profitably. That's the kind of enterprise that entrepreneurs can figure out better than you can. All you have to do is issue the challenge: Is capitalism capable of responding to this demand for a product? (Suppressed parenthesis: Or should the government move into this area?) Let the pros take it from there.

How does this differ from suggestion 41? Mainly in scale. In that discussion, you were talking to people who had only a few units to rent. Now you're approaching developers with questions like, Where are the service-industry people going to live in that new neighborhood you're developing? Not all of them will laugh at you. Some will see the plausibility of that consideration from financial and social-ethical standpoints.

44. Distinguish different homeless populations

Background

It has been well said that there are no simple solutions to simple problems; there are complex solutions to complex problems. If that's true, realizing the complexity of a problem is the first step in finding solutions rather than being an excuse for discouraged inaction.

In a previous section we noted that homeless people are not a problem; the shortage of affordable houses is the problem. Still people end up on the street for a welter of reasons, making the causality of homelessness a complexity indeed. Just building more low-cost housing will help a lot. (There's no point in building more units if they're priced off the market for low-income people—that may in fact require razing existing low-cost housing to build for yuppies.) However, building alone will not solve some of the problems. Eliminating crack cocaine will help a lot—but not entirely. Day care for working mothers' children will help a lot—if you're a working mother.

How to Do It

Sift through the stories you've been hearing. Figure out some categories, such as

- male/female
- child/adult/elderly
- single/families
- black/white/hispanic
- crack addicted/alcohol addicted/no known substance addictions
- mentally healthy/mentally impaired
- physically healthy/physically impaired
- employed/unemployed
- local/out of town
- skilled/unskilled
- education level
- how long on the street
- using shelters/personal care homes
- most options/fewest options

That list is not complete, nor does it reflect the reality of homelessness in all municipalities. The categories are not mutually exclusive since several can pertain to one person. But such a list will help you sift through the stories you're collecting.

Almost certainly you will find yourself more drawn to one element of the homeless population than to others. There is no problem with that. But this exercise will equip you to insert some sensible thinking into social chitchat, let alone political debate, when homelessness is discussed.

45. Explore the economics of homelessness

Background

Poverty is expensive. The United States cannot afford it. The bland (or despairing) assumption that there will always be an underclass beneath the national or local economy confines us to a future marked by more expensive (and unjust) law enforcement, higher public health expenditures, more public housing, and more government bureaucracy. A desirable future must include the poor in the cash economy. The more people who have a stake in the economy, the better off we all are.

As one who is probably in the economy yourself, you will have thoughts about how the poor can be cut into the action as you get to know some of them. Your thoughts can achieve high accuracy if you grasp what would be involved from the poor person's standpoint.

How to Do It

You don't have to be a former economics major to wade into this one. Nor do you need to gather a huge supply of information. Just some common sense will take you far.

Ask around among homeless people, among employers, among United Way workers, and among public servants until you can answer some of the following questions:

- In my town, are there labor pools?
- What does a laborer take home after a day in one of them?
- What does child care cost a working mother?
- What is the price of low-cost housing?
- What start-up costs and deposits are standard for that housing?
- What public transportation is available?
- What parts of town are not reachable by bus?
- What medical/dental/eye care is available for those not on public assistance?
- At what cost?
- What grocery stores are located nearby low-cost housing areas?
- How do the prices compare with those where I shop?
- What is the minimum wage?
- What jobs in my town pay minimum wage?

Again, the more you know, the more complex it seems. But take heart. Complex systems are the most vulnerable to change. Somewhere in the complexity there will be obvious things that you as an individual can do—and even more things you can do in concert with others. Don't duck the information; don't protect yourself from the real data. If you can let it all simmer in your brain while you stay in loving relationships with real street people, some adventurous projects and activities will start popping up. You will find yourself beginning to connect with other people who share your concerns. If the people you connect with have been out there longer

than you, you need one another; you need their information,
and they need your fresh energy, your enthusiasm, and your
objective ability to spot opportunities they are too close to
see.

46. Draw up an imaginary monthly budget based on minimum wage

Background

There's a lot to be said on both sides of the minimum wage debate. You don't have to ask about it much or read much about it to feel the force of several positions on it. Whatever your views on it, you will benefit by going through a simple exercise to get a notion of what minimum wage feels like to someone at the bottom of the job market. That information will make more urgent the task of elevating people's job and life skills and employment opportunities. It will also cut through much of the self-protective tendencies we all have to blame the victim.

How to Do It

From your talks with street people and with employers, get a rough figure for what a minimum wage worker actually takes home each week. Do it by the month if you like. (As of this writing, the minimum wage in Atlanta allows a worker to carry home $610 per month.) Consider some of the following questions and any others that occur to you:

- How much rent can I afford?
- How much for food?
- What can I afford to eat?
- What recreation or entertainment can I afford?
- How often?
- How will I get around?
- What if I get an abscessed molar?
- What if I get a kidney stone?
- What if I get a foot infection?
- Am I better off single or married?
- Can I afford children?
- Can I afford birth control?

You get the point.

The object of that exercise is not to make you feel bad or guilty. People don't undertake good acts on the basis of guilt; people do good acts for the fun of it. That really does need to be the basis of your efforts with street people if you're going to stick to them.

But the exercise should make your thinking more realistic. It may also make you less patient with the self-sparing folly that one hears talked concerning poverty at suburban parties.

47. Find out about rent structures in your locality

Background

If you apply this research to the fruit of the previous exercise, homelessness will begin to make more sense. For example, if you find that few private two-bedroom apartments are available for two hundred dollars per month, you can figure that few people on minimum wage can afford private housing.

You have already learned that homelessness has more than one cause. But one main cause is the lack of affordable housing for poor people. In getting to know some of them, you have met a number of them who are (or were) employed. It's not just laziness. Not all of them are substance abusers or spendthrifts. Much of the problem is that as bad as the real estate market is, it's still a seller's market.

When our parents were growing up, every town had one or more respectable boarding houses. Try to find one in your vicinity today. There used to be stable neighborhoods where lower income people lived. Today many of those have been leveled for freeways, athletic stadia, shopping malls, high-rise (and high-cost) apartments, or business districts.

In smaller towns you can see the evolution still taking place. Former residential houses on main streets are being used as offices by small-time lawyers, chiropractors, real estate dealers, and palm readers, all interspersed with fast-food franchises and used car lots. Closer to town (or further away), shopping plazas and eventually malls show up on what were clearly residential acres in recent decades.

If you're not very well-off, where do you live?

How to Do It

From the privacy of your home, you can call numbers you find in the newspaper advertising housing. Act like a poor person on the low income you've already practiced.

Call a bank, asking to discuss a residential loan on some property in a district you know to be poor. Time anything from hard-boiled eggs to a standing rib roast by the time you spend on hold.

A friend who sells real estate can show you how to discover who owns particular properties that catch your eye as poorly maintained or overpriced. You may be surprised to discover names you know from other connections, such as fellow club members.

All this will equip you with information you cannot do much with as an individual. But you are a citizen. In concert with others, reacting to accurate analyses of the homeless situation, you can get a lot catalyzed. Coalitions of people with your concerns are already out there, after all.

48. Learn all you can about addictive disease

Background

Though not all homeless people are on the street because of drug or alcohol addiction, you have surely encountered any number who fall into that category. Addiction is complex and difficult to understand, in individuals, in a family, and in the whole society. It raises not-yet-settled questions pertaining to our national and local resolution to seal off the supply of legal and illegal substances to which people addict themselves—all that gets tricky when you consider that illegal substances may be this country's major consumer products.

Nobody who remains ignorant of addictive disease can take an intelligent role in any discussion of modern society. This is especially true when attempting to get into the situations of homeless people.

An earlier suggestion was that you try to sort some of the homeless people you meet into groupings. In the locality from which this book emerges, the following can be readily distinguished:

- people just come to town for work, using the shelters or streets while they get their bearings
- families who have just lost one of two incomes
- people paying more than 70 percent of their incomes for rent
- single mothers with children who are not getting child support
- inmates of prisons or mental hospitals recently released
- alcoholics (comprising many combat veterans)
- crack cocaine addicts

Addiction shows up in more than one of those populations. Anyone who stays on the street long enough is at great risk.

How to Do It

There is no lack of information available on addiction. Your phone directory will contain a general number for Alcoholics Anonymous, a source of some of the best and most reliable information. Many churches and synagogues now sponsor recovery groups and educational programs; most pastors and rabbis can supply information on addiction, as can your physician.

I recommend reading *Addiction and Grace* by Gerald R. May, M.D. Dr. May's discussion will put you in touch with some of your own (no doubt less harmful) addictions. (Did you know you can addict yourself easily to nose drops?) Identifying your addictions will lend understanding and a measure of sympathy for crack addicts and alcoholics—however offensive their behavior when they are under the influence.

You simply *must not* do one thing in learning about addiction. Leave all illegal drugs alone, even experimentally. Most especially, consider any experiment with crack the way you'd consider a round of Russian roulette with players who owe you money. People who have tried crack as well as other drugs report that its addictive powers are difficult to exaggerate. One addicted friend told this writer, "Go ahead; try it. Then start your clock. You'll be down here on the street before six months go by." Several journalists' families can testify to the tragic reliability of that advice.

49. Help homeless people into a worshiping community

Background

This suggestion makes all kinds of sense. Religious communities have much to offer homeless people. They have clothes, cars, a certain amount of money (e.g., for a deposit on an apartment), counsel for personal difficulties, financial counseling, members with empty rooms in their houses, people with extra furniture and appliances, a tax-free registration that allows people to make gifts, and so forth. They also have an ideology (theology, doctrine) that says they are supposed to be doing a certain amount of these things already.

It cannot be too often repeated that homelessness is a symptom of the breakdown of human community. Connecting homeless people with a community begins a reversal of our pervading social illness. Love and care (human and divine) lie close to the heart of most religious congregations, however awkwardly they are expressed. Homeless people don't get a lot of love, but they certainly need it.

Any congregation that gets involved with homeless people will have encouraging stories of street people getting back on their feet as a result of individuals or groups taking an interest in them.

No congregation can clean up homelessness single-handedly. But individual congregations can help people back up one by one with much less effort and cost than people expect.

How to Do It

Consider two candidate communities. The first, of course, is your own. The advantages to that are three.

- You can take them yourself.
- You know the people to introduce them to.
- You can lead them through the service.

But there are some disadvantages to long-term reliance on your congregation. They include

- transportation
- class differences and reciprocal shyness

Still, taking them to your own services is a good start. Don't worry much on the front end about doctrinal, denominational, or even religious differences. The duty to a poor neighbor is fairly widespread. And the place will feel so new and frightening to your friends, it'll be a while before they feel like arguing over or disputing doctrines.

The other candidate congregation is one representing the group in which your friends grew up. There are some advantages, such as

- transportation
- previous cultural familiarity

The difficulties may include

- embarrassment at returning in this condition
- inhospitality
- your inability to introduce them to someone you know

Some low-income congregations may resist integrating street people, seeing them as having succumbed to temptations that they themselves have successfully resisted. There's no sense in arguing with that attitude; simply try another group.

But however you decide to proceed, this will almost certainly prove a life-giving service to your friends.

50. Organize a health clinic for homeless people

Background

You have already seen the pressing need for health and dental care among street people. A little bit goes a long way. For example, just periodic foot care makes an essential difference to people without cars and people who have to work standing up. There is great need for convalescent care and physical therapy for poor people recovering from surgery, injuries, and illnesses. Prenatal care can reduce some of the overwhelming public costs we're all going to be paying taxes against in the coming decades, since we have permitted the proliferation of an economic underclass, because some of the children won't come into the world brain damaged or addicted.

You have also seen the hassle street people go through to access the care already available to them: waiting on transportation and service, for example.

What you may not have seen is the willingness of physicians, nurses, dentists, and dental hygienists to help out.

When the need and the resources get together, it can be really exciting.

How to Do It

First, see if a shelter you're connected with or some other downtown religious group will offer space for a clinic. Usually we're not talking about full-time but only a day a week or some portion of it—at least initially.

Next, talk the idea up with your own physician, your dentist, physical therapists, and other health providers. Ask them who would support such an idea.

As you talk about the idea, it will be clear that you are not opening a center for brain surgery or heart transplants. But that's not what's needed. Poor people need the sort of thing you can go to your own health care providers for with relatively little thought or cost, prevention as much as cure.

Expect to be gratified by how the idea catches on. The people you're buttonholing originally went into their professions to be helpful to people and often seek a way to make their services available to the poor. Physicians and dentists who have practiced in military service will often have fascinating ideas about what can be done with simple equipment.

51. Pray for your street friends

Background

Among the many good reasons for this suggestion, consider the following ones.

First, in a way we understand, praying helps another person in that it opens your heart to him. If you pray for a person with any regularity, chances are that you'll stick with her. You will find this motivates you, preventing burnout, offering an expression for the griefs you'll encounter and feel, inspiring you when you're too tired to keep an engagement with a street person.

Second, prayer helps the other person in ways that we don't really understand. But generations of people in all cultures, some of them wise, testify that prayer is efficient behavior. Some journalists once asked an archbishop of Canterbury, a prominent theologian, to discuss the purpose of prayer, then they braced themselves for a weighty, lengthy reply. To their surprise, he answered simply, "When I pray, coincidences happen; when I quit praying, coincidences quit happening."

Third, praying for your friends on the streets may get you

praying about other matters. It may get you praying, period. You will find that does you good.

Fourth, though it is normally done in private, prayer is public; it reaches out to a wider community with your concern and affection. Though it's often done quietly, it's an action; it forms and solidifies the human community. Some of us sense that in some way it participates in solidifying the whole cosmos.

Well, the cosmic aspect is great and all that, but our object is to offer some real, specific help to some real, specific people. Prayer makes sense toward that object because it allows the meaning of what we're doing—what we're "called" to do, some would insist—to catch up with us and nourish us. That arms us in the face of the sense of futility that prevents any action whatever. Simply put, prayer keeps us on the job.

How to Do It

There seems no universally preferred way to hold your mouth or hands in praying. Perhaps the religious groups you've bumped into in your time with your street friends contain some people who give evidence of the kind of interior life you'd like to cultivate; ask them how they do it. The teachers in your congregations may have some preferred ways they recommend. But no area of life is more fruitful for your personal experiments.

Postures include kneeling (if it helps), sitting, lying down on your stomach or back, standing, or pacing.

You can do it aloud, as in a conversation. You can do it quietly, as an internal conversation. Or you can simply use images, such as seeing your friends surrounded with Light or handing them into the lap of God. You can simply whisper their names. You can write letters to God about them. You can journal about them. Really, it's more important that you start doing something you recognize as prayer for your friends than that you do it "right." Prayer is one of the few areas of life in which intention counts more than proficiency.

Instead of asking this discussion to talk you into thinking prayer is efficient, why not make your own experiment? Pray for your friend in whatever manner feels most natural to you. Pay attention to what develops in his or her life. Pay attention to shifts in your understanding, boosts in your energy, and your own sense of connectedness.

52. Write about your experiences with homeless people

Background

If you've read this far, you know the point of this suggestion. People want to know what's going on and what they can do about it. This is a crucial time to show people that they really can do some things that will make a difference to people who need the difference made. Writing for publication is a good way to get that done. If you've tried even some of the suggestions so far, you already have a lot to write about.

How to Do It

Getting somebody to print what you write is not all that difficult. You probably belong to a half-dozen organizations that publish newsletters. If you know the editors of those publications, you're familiar with the hollow-eyed stare that disfigures their faces as publication time approaches. They need interesting copy. They will publish *anything*. You are their answer, the solution to their problem. Don't neglect your local paper. Alumni publications like first-person articles from their graduates.

What you represent is not necessarily special virtue (posturing that way would embarrass most of us); it's not expertise, either (you now know that you know less than you knew at first because you know so much more). What you represent is *stories*. You know some folks you didn't know before, people you can describe with warmth. You've been blinded with tears by some display of courage that seems superhuman, by acts of generosity that would shame any philanthropist, by hard luck that ought not to happen to Nero.

People need to hear the stories. They profess our kinship with each other, a relatedness that we are lost if we ignore. As you tell your stories—or those of your friends—the torn tissues of human community gets drawn back toward health and integrity.

Afterword

Even if you've arrived this far, chances are that you haven't done very much with the suggestions. Even if you've worked your way to this point, you have found that some of them just aren't open to you. Be assured that I have not done all of them, either, though somebody or other I know has done everything mentioned.

So this may be a profitable place to review a few basic principles.

First, renew your renunciation of guilt. In a fourth-century Easter sermon attributed to John Chrysostom, we read the following:

> O you that have wearied yourselves in fasting and you who have neglected the fast, rejoice together; o you ascetics and you lazy, rejoice together. To the one God gives, to the other he is generous; God both loves the act and praises the intention!

In other words, congratulate yourself that you've read a small book on the topic up to this page. Yes, that's hard to imagine. But any attempt to respond to homeless people that is not rooted in something like that spirit will lead to personal vanity and eventual burnout.

Second, the more difficult and complex tasks get easier if you're faithful with the little tasks. All of it is based on getting to know some homeless people and staying in periodic touch with them. The rest flows out of a few fundamental relationships that become friendships.

Third, honor your journal. It has at least three values. If you want to assist others in their service to or relationships with homeless people, you will have stored a lot of insights in it that you can use. (Remember not to share the actual pages; they're private, for your eyes only.)

Your journal of this project is a record of your growth and change. The Yiddish language offers Jewish people lovely compliments to offer others; perhaps its finest is *mensch*, which means a fully "human being," one with integrity. Your journal is the record of how you became a *mensch*. Honor it.

You will discover (only if you have kept it strictly private) that your journal is a conversation between two spirits. The one, of course, is yourself. The other is the Spirit of God. For thousands of years people have discerned that Spirit at work in creation, in nature, and in human affairs. Now He's there on your pages. That is what all these experiments and efforts among homeless people have been about. Your friends on the street have known that since shortly after they got there. Now you have got there yourself. And you know it, too.

Gray Temple, Jr., has served as chairman of the Joint Urban Ministries Committee and is rector of St. Patrick's Episcopal Church in Atlanta, Georgia. He serves as chaplain and honorary captain to the Atlanta Police Bureau and as campus pastor at Appalachian State University. Temple has conducted teaching seminars in Burma, India, Pakistan, the U.K., and Kenya. In 1990, Temple had a sabbatical during which time he studied the problems of the homeless in Metro Atlanta.